fearless in the cause

Related Works

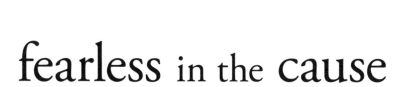

fearless in the cause

Remarkable Stories from Women in Church History

Edited by Brittany Chapman Nash and Richard E. Turley Jr.

DESERET
BOOK

Salt Lake City, Utah

Library of Congress Cataloging-in-Publication Data

Names: Nash, Brittany Chapman, editor. | Turley, Richard E., Jr., 1956– editor.
Title: Fearless in the cause: remarkable stories from women in Church history / edited by Brittany Chapman Nash and Richard E. Turley Jr.
Description: Salt Lake City, Utah : Deseret Book, [2016] | ?2016 |
Selections from Women of faith in the latter days, edited by Richard E. Turley Jr. and Brittany A. Chapman (Salt Lake City : Deseret Book, 2011–2014). | Includes bibliographical references and index.
Identifiers: LCCN 2015038542 | ISBN 9781629720241 (hardbound : alk. paper)
Subjects: LCSH: Mormon women—Biography. | The Church of Jesus Christ of Latter-day Saints—Biography. | LCGFT: Biographies.
Classification: LCC BX8693 .S76 2016 | DDC 289.3092/52—dc23
LC record available at http://lccn.loc.gov/2015038542

Printed in the United States of America
RR Donnelley, Crawfordsville, IN

10   9   8   7   6   5   4   3   2

Contents

A Note to the Reader

This volume of stories contains highlights from the first three volumes of *Women of Faith in the Latter Days,* works that tell the stories of women in The Church of Jesus Christ of Latter-day Saints. Though their experiences vary, these women are united in their testimonies of the gospel of Jesus Christ and their commitment to it. The projected seven-volume series begins with some of the earliest Latter-day Saint women and will culminate in the stories of living women around the globe.

The volumes of *Women of Faith in the Latter Days* are organized by birth year of the women whose stories are included. The women in the first volume were born before or in 1820, the first generation of Mormon women. Many lived through the persecution of the Kirtland, Missouri, and Nauvoo eras, and their memoirs are stirring and humbling, filled with the fiery faith of those discovering a new religion just gaining a foothold in the world.

The women whose stories are told in volume 2 (1821–1845) may have seen those early scenes of persecution as children or adolescents; many were converts from the British Isles, Scandinavia, and Australia. They accepted the principle of "the gathering" with courage, crossing the plains and settling the desert lands of North America's Intermountain West.

The women of volume 3 (1846–1870) include second-generation Saints who were born to Latter-day Saint parents and raised in Mormon settlements that stretched from Canada to Mexico. Converts also hailed from farther-flung regions of the world. The women in this volume began to extend themselves in a wider sphere of service and advocated for women's rights, greater opportunities in education, and such political causes as women's suffrage. They joined hands with national and international women's leaders, including Susan B. Anthony.

Each chapter, both in this volume and in the main volumes of the series, is written by a different author. We cast a net far and wide to solicit chapters and invited anyone to submit a chapter (and still do for upcoming volumes). Some of the authors are professional historians; others have never been previously published. All have dug through a kaleidoscope of sources to enrich their narratives; records come from journals, reminiscences, autobiographies, correspondence, memoirs, and oral history interviews. We and the authors have been sticklers for acquiring original records where possible in order to ensure faithful accuracy to the stories of the women featured. Where possible, we have tried to reflect each woman's own voice because no one can tell her story as well as she can.

In all three volumes are women we love as friends and view with awe. They have tutored us with the wisdom of years—wisdom often gained at a price—and they have enlarged our hearts and strengthened our faith. Through these women, we understand a bit more the convictions that fueled their sense of purpose amidst trial and the joys and testimonies that kept them true to the faith. We hope you enjoy learning more about the women upon whose shoulders we stand, who consecrated all, and who have reached beyond what they could see.

A LEGACY OF COURAGE

A Borrowed Mirror

SUSANAH STONE LLOYD

Susanah Stone was born on Christmas Eve 1830 in Bristol, England. When she was eighteen years old, she became the first of her family to join the Church, followed a few months later by her younger sister, Sarah, and later still, her mother. Contrary to her parents' wishes, however, Susanah desired to gather with the Saints. She gained employment with a man who was generous with her wages, and she was able to save enough to pay for the journey. In May 1856, at age twenty-five, Susanah left Liverpool, England, with a group of Saints aboard the ship *Thornton* bound for New York. The party was directed by Captain James Willie.

The Willie and Martin handcart companies faced more adversity from weather and death than did any other Latter-day Saint companies during the pioneer migration west. As the only member of her family in the Willie company, Susanah found support from devoted friends on the trail. The single women traveled together, pulling their handcarts during the day and sharing two tents at night. They did all they could to aid and encourage each other.

The arduous journey was made more difficult by the loss of a substantial number of cattle, scarce provisions, fear of Indian attacks, and extreme weather. Traveling with scant clothing and lacking sufficient food, they suffered greatly from the severe cold and snow. In an autobiographical sketch written five years before her death, Susanah recalled, "We waded thru the cold streams many times but we murmured not for our faith in God and our testimony of His work were supreme. And in the blizzards and falling snow we sat under our hand carts and sang, 'Come, come, ye Saints, no toil nor labor fear, but with joy wend your way.'"[1]

Susanah had suitors both in England and in her handcart company, but she had been advised not to marry before reaching Salt Lake. The advice proved to be well-founded. Her suitor in the handcart company, Theophilus Cox, with whom she had also kept company in England, died on the trail and was buried on the plains, as were many others.

Only once did Susanah's courage fail. Her feet were frostbitten, and one cold, dreary afternoon, she felt she could go no farther. Susanah withdrew from her group and sat down to await the end, feeling as if she was in a stupor. She later wrote, "After a time I was aroused by a voice, which seemed as audible as anything could be, and which spoke to my very soul of the promises and blessings I had received, and which should surely be fulfilled and that I had a mission to perform in Zion. I received strength and was filled with the Spirit of the Lord and arose and traveled on with a light heart."[2]

When she reached the camp, Susanah discovered that a search party was gathered, ready to go back and find her, dead or alive. Although her frostbitten feet continued to give her trouble for many years to come, at the end of her life Susanah wrote that it was a small price to pay "in the contemplation of the many blessings the gospel has brought to me and mine."[3]

When the Willie company was about a hundred miles from the Salt Lake Valley, their captain dreamed that a rescue group was coming from the valley to meet them. His dream was prophetic: volunteer teamsters soon arrived with provisions to help the company complete their journey. Less than three weeks later, they had nearly reached Salt Lake City. After months on the plains and the extreme hardships they had endured, Susanah and her companions

tried to make themselves as presentable as possible to greet old friends who would be welcoming them into the valley. Susanah recalled, "I had sold my little looking glass to the Indians for buffalo meat, so I borrowed one and I shall never forget how I looked. Some of my old friends did not know me. We were so weather beaten and tanned."[4]

Among those who came to meet the Willie company was Thomas Lloyd, a handsome young man who had migrated to Utah the previous year from Wolverhampton, England. His parents had died when he was a child, and he was raised by a wealthy aunt who had never married. Thomas stood to inherit her fortune, but his aunt cut him off when he refused to renounce his new Mormon faith. Soon after Susanah reached the valley, and on the advice of President Brigham Young, she and Thomas were married. The couple settled in Farmington, where Thomas provided for their family by making saddles and harnesses. Eventually they moved to Wellsville to secure more land for their growing family, which expanded to include ten sons and four daughters. Just as she had as a handcart pioneer, Susanah "traveled on, trusting in God," throughout her life.[5]

Almost 150 years after the Willie handcart company crossed the plains under the harshest of conditions, Relief Society general president Mary Ellen Smoot recounted Susanah's experience of borrowing a mirror at her journey's end and not being able to recognize herself. Sister Smoot observed that Susanah "was a different person, both inside and out. Over the course of rocky ridges and extreme hardship came a deep conviction. Her faith had been tried, and her conversion was concrete. She had been refined in ways that the very best mirror could not reflect. Susanna had prayed for strength and found it—deep within her soul."[6]

From "I Hailed It with Joy," by David R. Cook, in *Women of Faith in the Latter Days, Volume Two, 1821–1845*, edited by Richard E. Turley Jr. and Brittany A. Chapman (Salt Lake City: Deseret Book, 2012), 183–95.

Fearless in the Cause

LAURA CLARK PHELPS

Newly converted to the restored gospel, Laura Clark Phelps and her husband, Morris, gathered with the Saints to Jackson County, Missouri, in March 1832. There, in a borrowed tent, Laura gave birth to their third child, a daughter that family lore claims was the first Mormon girl to be born in Independence.[1] The Phelps family was soon driven with the rest of the Saints from Jackson County into Clay County and finally to Far West, Missouri.

As persecution against the Saints escalated, confrontations with mobbers became increasingly harsh. Laura's daughter Mary Ann recalled: "They [the mobbers] would even come into her yard and shoot the chickens and kill the pigs. Mother had her house full of women and children, in the mean time, who had been driven from their homes by the enemy. These women wanted mother to go into the woods to escape the mob, but she told them 'No,' that if she had to die, she would die in her own home, so they decided to stay with her."[2]

During those dark and threatening times in 1838, Laura's husband, Morris, was arrested and thrown into the Richmond Jail with Parley P. Pratt and four others while Joseph and Hyrum Smith and five others were taken to Liberty Jail. Laura's daughter Mary Ann noted: "Father was told many times that if he would burn his Mormon Bible and quit the Mormon Church he could go free . . . but he chose to be firm in his religion; so he was held in prison all winter, and mother had to support her family the best way she could; her provisions and every thing had been destroyed by the armies."[3]

Amazingly under such circumstances, Laura managed to visit her husband every two weeks and take him provisions so he had something to eat besides the prison food that was often inedible. On one of those occasions, she discovered that Heber C. Kimball had also come to visit the prisoners. He recalled the event in his journal: "On our arrival at Richmond, I went directly to the prison to see Parley, but was prohibited by the guard, who said they would blow my brains out if I attempted to go near him. In a few minutes, Sister Morris Phelps came to me in great agitation and advised me to leave forthwith, as Brother Pratt had told her that a large body of men had assembled with tar, feathers and a rail, who swore they would tar and feather me, and ride me on the rail."[4]

Elder Kimball later expounded: "When my life was sought at Richmond, and my brethren in prison had great anxiety on my account, she interceded with my pursuers, who were nearly thirty in number, and actually convinced them that I was another person, altogether, and the pursuit was stopped."[5] Laura's courageous spirit may have saved his life.

After Governor Lilburn W. Boggs issued the infamous exter-mination order, Laura packed up her children and what few pos-sessions she could and left Missouri. With her husband still in jail, she drove a wagon from Far West, Missouri, across the Mississippi River to Quincy and then Commerce, Illinois, and then back across the Mississippi to Montrose, Iowa, where her family settled in an abandoned building that had been used to stable horses.

Despite the distance, Laura was determined to return to Missouri to see her husband and attend his trial. Her brother, John Wesley Clark, joined her for the 150-mile journey on horseback. They arrived in Columbia, Boone County, Missouri, where Morris, Parley P. Pratt, and King Follett had been transferred. Laura found that Orson Pratt, brother of Parley, had also come to attend the court proceedings. They yearned for the freedom of their fam-ily members, and the Lord had a plan for their liberation. Parley

recorded that before Orson and Laura arrived, "the Lord had shown me in a vision of the night the manner and means of escape [from jail]. Mrs. Phelps had the same thing shown to her in a vision previous to her arrival."[6]

The daring escape attempt required great courage and resolve. The plan was for Laura to arrange boarding for a few weeks with the family of the jail keeper, who occupied part of the building that held the prison. This served the double purpose of lowering the jail keeper's guard and making Laura's horse available (along with her brother John's horse and Orson Pratt's horse) for the three prisoners to make their escape.

The breakout was carefully planned. The prisoners were to await the opening of their upstairs cell door by the jailer. Parley P. Pratt recounted the strategy:

"Mr. Follett was to give the door a sudden pull, and fling it wide open the moment the key was turned. Mr. Phelps being well skilled in wrestling was to press out foremost, and come in contact with the jailer; I was to follow in the centre, and Mr. Follett, who held the door, was to bring up the rear, while sister Phelps was to pray."[7] Laura's daughter related the adventure:

"Mother said she sat back on the bed in the kitchen, and pretty soon she could hear steps and a rumbling noise, heard the jailer call out, and she said his wife rushed up stairs to where he was (she weighed about two hundred pounds.) The jailer had father clinched, but father jumped down two pair of stairs, six steps each, and with the jailer's wife hanging on to one of his arms. He would get rid of her when he jumped, but she would clinch him again when she again reached him. . . . Mother said . . . she thought she could pray if she could do nothing else. She thought she was whispering a prayer, but they said she hollered just as loud as her voice would let her, and she said, 'Oh! Thou God of Abraham, Isaac and Jacob, deliver Thy Servant.' Father said he felt as strong as a giant when he heard those words; he just pushed the jailer and his wife off as if they were babies and cleared himself."[8]

Meanwhile, Orson and Laura's brother John held the horses at the agreed-upon meeting point. Morris and Parley were able to get away, but King Follett was captured on Laura's horse, which was strong evidence of her participation in the plot. As news of the escape spread, Laura faced alone the wrath of a mob who gathered around the prison.

It is remarkable that Laura chose to remain at the scene, her own life at risk. According to Parley: "They threatened her with instant death, and finally turned her out of doors in the dusk of the evening. . . . Being a stranger and without money, friends, or acquaintances in the place, she knew not where to go or what to do. She finally sat down in the open air in the midst of the mob, by whom she was assailed, cursed, insulted, threatened, and abused in the most unfeeling manner for some time."[9]

A little boy who witnessed the scene heard the jailer threaten to "put [Laura] out of the way" if she were not gone by dark.[10] The boy ran home and returned with his parents, who were appalled at the cruelty directed at Laura. The Richardson family took pity on her and gave her refuge in their home.

They proved to be true friends. The next day they returned to the jail and collected items belonging to Morris. They searched until they found Laura's sidesaddle, which the mobbers had vandalized. After a few days, Mr. Richardson located her horse, which had been abused by the mob in their pursuit of Morris and Parley after the recapture of King Follett. Mr. Richardson repaired the saddle and nursed the horse back to health. Laura's daughter Mary Ann recorded, "Mother stayed with these good people ten days; never heard a word as to whether father was dead or alive, but mother was a woman with lots of faith and courage."[11]

Laura was determined to return to her family in Iowa, despite the Richardsons' concerns about the dangers for a woman traveling alone through unsettled country where bandits roamed. Finally, they all agreed that Laura would travel a good part of the way with the mail boy, setting out early in the morning and riding late into the night. Leaving the Richardsons with a Book of Mormon and a hymnbook, Laura began the journey.

Traveling alone for the last leg of her journey, Laura entered an area of thick woods just as darkness began to fall. Her daughter wrote, "She said this was the first time her courage failed her, she had such a lonesome, dismal feeling come over her . . . and she did not know what would accost her."[12] Then, amazingly, she saw a man approaching on horseback. It proved to be King Follett's son who had been sent to find out if Laura had ended up in prison because no one had heard from her. Together they traveled to Quincy, Illinois, where Morris was recovering from his eight months in prison and three days without food or rest during his escape. Laura also found that Orson Pratt and her brother John had safely arrived there after walking more than a hundred miles from Columbia, Missouri. King Follett was eventually released from jail several months after his recapture on account of his age and his not being considered a Church leader.

Laura and Morris still feared for Morris's safety and did not dare stay long with the kind people of Quincy. After only a few days, they left their children with neighbors and traveled to Kirtland, Ohio, to visit Morris's family. They attempted to teach his Phelps relatives the gospel but to no avail.

After a lengthy time away from Illinois, the family was re-united in July 1840, but their season of happiness was short-lived. Laura's daughter Mary Ann recalled: "We moved to a town twenty miles from Nauvoo called Masedonia, here we located and soon all were our friends. . . . We lived there about a year and a half, which were the happiest days of our lives; then my mother was taken sick and died, leaving her five children, three girls and two boys, the baby one and a half years old. We were all heartbroken and did not know how to manage without mother. She was buried in Nauvoo. . . . Hard work and exposure had broken her health."[13]

Among the many tributes given at Laura's funeral, Heber C. Kimball said, "She was one of the first who embraced the gospel . . . [and] manifested to the world that no sacrifice was too great for her to make for the cause which she had espoused."[14] The Prophet Joseph Smith said "her salvation was sure."[15] An entry about her in the compiled *History of the Church* concluded simply, "Her rest is glorious."[16]

From "Tried like Gold," by Carol L. Clark, in *Women of Faith in the Latter Days, Volume One, 1775–1820*, edited by Richard E. Turley Jr. and Brittany A. Chapman (Salt Lake City: Deseret Book, 2011), eBook.

Shipwrecked

ROSA CLARA FRIEDLANDER LOGIE

I n the 1840s, a voyage by sailing ship from England to the British colony of New South Wales (Australia) was long and hazardous; however, thousands of emigrants gladly risked the dangers in hope of a better life. Among them were eleven-year-old Rosa Clara Friedlander, her widowed mother, Eliza, and Rosa's eight-year-old brother, James.

By the time the Friedlander family arrived in Sydney, the town that had been founded as a penal settlement in 1788 was a thriving metropolis trying to forget its convict origins. When the first Latter-day Saint missionaries from America arrived in 1851, fifteen-year-old Rosa and her family were among their early converts.

A year later, at age sixteen, Rosa married another Latter-day Saint convert, Charles Joseph Gordon Logie, a New Zealander who had gone to sea in his late teens. One day Charles, then in his early twenties, found himself on shore leave in Sydney. According to Logie family history, Charles and a group of sailor friends were walking along a Sydney street when they spotted beautiful young

Rosa Friedlander on the upstairs balcony of a Latter-day Saint meeting place. Charles reportedly declared, "I'm going to marry that girl," and climbed up the supporting posts and introduced himself to her.[1] Soon he was taught the gospel and was baptized.

Shortly thereafter, he and Rosa were married. But since Latter-day Saint elders were not legally authorized to perform marriages in Australia at that time, Charles and Rosa were married at the Scots Church in Pitt Street, Sydney, by the well-known Presbyterian minister, the Reverend James Fullerton, an outspoken opponent of the Mormon missionaries.

Mission president Augustus A. Farnham and Mary Ann Gingell, another Latter-day Saint branch member, signed the marriage register as a witnesses. President Farnham recorded in his journal that on "May 21 Saturday . . . attended the wedding of Bro Logie and Sister Rose Clara Freelander at Parson Fullerton's. Returned to Bro Gangels [Gingell's] and married them over again."[2] Friends from the Sydney Branch then enjoyed a small reception for the young couple in the home of William and Mary Gingell.

The Saints in Sydney, like converts in Europe, longed to gather with the Latter-day Saints in Zion. Charles and Rosa made plans to sail with a group of Church members to California en route to the Salt Lake Valley. The vessel, *Julia Ann,* was relatively new and had successfully taken an earlier company of Latter-day Saints on the same voyage. Charles, an experienced sailor, was hired on as a crew member to work for his passage. He and Rosa and their one-year-old daughter, Annie Augusta (whom they had named in honor of President Farnham), were among the fifty-six people on board, twenty-eight of whom were Latter-day Saints. The ship left Sydney Harbour on September 7, 1855.

Life on board proceeded smoothly and harmoniously for the first month of the journey. Then, on the evening of October 3, the *Julia Ann* violently struck a reef near the atoll then known as the Scilly Isles, some 340 miles west of Tahiti.[3] Investigations later found that although the captain's calculations were correct, the navigation chart was inaccurate, and the vessel was actually sixty to ninety miles off course.[4]

It quickly became obvious that the tilting vessel was badly damaged and taking on water. Huge waves broke over the ship, which shuddered with each impact so the passengers found it almost impossible to stand. At first all was confusion and terror in the tropical darkness, but one of the sailors, an expert swimmer, managed to swim to the reef and secure a rope. Back on board, the captain fashioned a sling, and one of the crew prepared to take the women and children off the sinking ship one by one.

Not knowing what awaited them, young Rosa bravely volunteered to go first. She helped tie baby Annie securely to Charles's back in a brown woolen shawl and readied herself to be taken to the reef.[5] Suddenly a giant wave smashed onto the stricken vessel, and Rosa watched in horror as her husband and baby were swept overboard.

Despite having been a sailor for several years, Charles did not know how to swim. A brave seaman dived into the pounding surf and grasped Charles by the hair, rescuing both him and Annie. Rosa courageously climbed onto the lap of a sailor seated in the sling and held on tight as they were hauled through the crashing waves to the reef by the sailors already there. Throughout the night, more passengers were ferried from the ship, where they were left standing in the darkness on the sharp coral reef, waist deep in water as the surf broke relentlessly over them.[6]

Others were not as fortunate. Two young Latter-day Saint girls were washed overboard and drowned, and two other Church members and a six-week-old baby were drowned in the flooded cabin. The ship then broke in two, and the heavier part of the vessel, weighed down by its cargo of coal, sank immediately. The lighter section of the vessel—with some of the migrating Saints still clinging to it—was washed high onto the reef, or more lives would have been lost. Thus, by midnight, the rest of the ship's company had arrived safely on the reef by means of either the rope and sling or the washed-up wreckage.

Daylight revealed an islet a few miles away. Over the next two days, the stranded survivors, bruised from being tossed around when the ship struck the reef and bleeding from cuts caused by the sharp coral, were ferried to safety on the islet in one of the ship's boats that had been saved from the wreck. This could not be done quickly, and some of the crew waited on the reef for two days, without food or water and exposed to the fierce tropical sun, until all the passengers had been moved. At last everyone reached the little island.

The survivors soon organized a daily routine. They filtered brackish water by placing a salvaged barrel in a hole dug in the sand. Their principal food was turtle meat and eggs, crabs, and some fish and coconuts. Little was salvaged from the ship—a few tools, a small amount of flour and other food, and a chest containing women's clothing. The survivors fashioned coconut shells into drinking vessels, one of which Rosa kept for the rest of her life. Except for minor injuries received on the night of the shipwreck, most of the castaways remained well, apart from boils exacerbated by their unorthodox diet.

There was little shelter to be had on the small islet where they were now camped until the men built some huts from wood and pandanus leaves. In the meantime, from the salvaged chest of clothing Charles fashioned a large silk skirt into a tent to shelter Rosa and Annie.

After several weeks, the crew managed to repair the ship's boat, and a few sailors, the ship's captain, and Latter-day Saint John McCarthy set out on November 20 to row more than two hundred miles to the nearest inhabited islands. Four days later, they reached Bora Bora and reported the tragedy. With the help of the British consul on the island of Rauatei, the captain of the schooner *Emma Packer* departed the next day for the tiny island refuge of the stranded *Julia Ann* company. On December 3, after two months of living as castaways, the survivors were rescued. They arrived in Papeete, the capital of the French Protectorate of Tahiti, on December 19, 1855.

Their troubles were not yet over, however. The travelers had paid their passage to San Francisco and did not have the money to pay again. In desperation, they appealed to both the British and American consuls in Papeete. Peter Penfold, writing to his brother in Australia, reported the result: "The American consul said that he had nothing to do with us, because we were English; and the English Consul said he had nothing to do with us, because we were in an American ship; so we were in a very peculiar situation,—without friends, without money, without home, without clothes, without food, and in a strange land, under the French Government." They could do little to help themselves and their families. "There is but very little work for a man to do in this place," Peter lamented.[7]

But true Christian charity eventually prevailed. Members of the local Freemasons Lodge heard of the survivors' plight and cared for the destitute emigrants until the consuls received authorization to

help their own nationals.[8] Over the next few weeks and months, all the survivors finally found passage aboard vessels bound for California. In March 1856, John Penfold, president of the company of Saints on the *Julia Ann*, wrote to mission president Augustus Farnham in Sydney, "Brother Logie, wife and child is about to sail for San Francisco in about a fortnight."[9] Seven months after the shipwreck—and eight months after sailing from Sydney—Charles and Rosa reached San Francisco by way of Honolulu. It was another year before the family finally arrived in Utah, where they ultimately settled in American Fork.

Rosa's singular empathy for weary wayfarers was evident throughout the remainder of her life. Her home was always open to travelers and became a regular stopping place for Saints journeying to and from general conference in Salt Lake City. One of her prized possessions was a small pewter teapot given to her by President George Q. Cannon in recognition of her bravery in being the first woman to leave the *Julia Ann* to go to the reef.

From "Hope in the Gospel," by Marjorie Newton, in *Women of Faith in the Latter Days, Volume Two, 1821–1845*, edited by Richard E. Turley Jr. and Brittany A. Chapman (Salt Lake City: Deseret Book, 2012), 196–209.

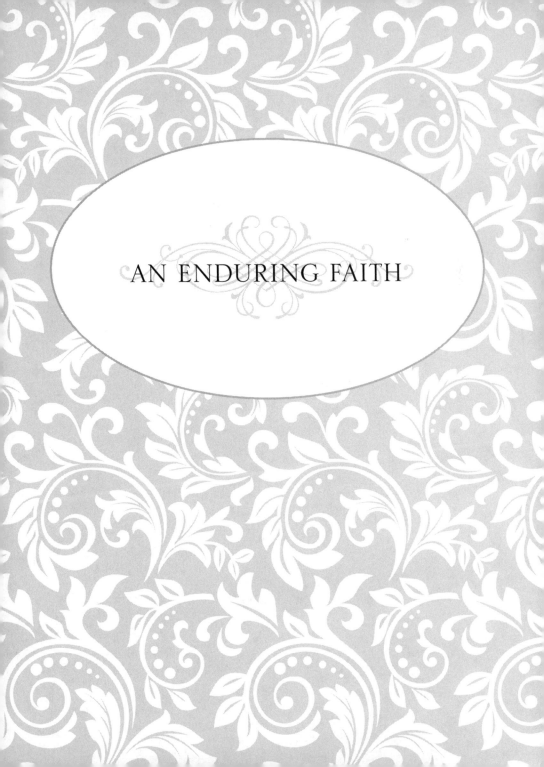

AN ENDURING FAITH

"It Was a Hard Struggle"

MARY ROSELIA COOK McCANN

Mary Roselia Cook was twenty years old when she and Hyrum McCann were married in 1883. Hyrum was the sole support of his widowed mother, widowed sister, and young niece. Because of these obligations, Mary and Hyrum intended to marry at a later time. However, when Hyrum sustained a serious leg injury that threatened his life, Mary knew they should be married right away.

"His mother was old and could not take care of him," she reasoned, "and his sister was handicapped in such a way that she could not either." Although the doctor warned that Hyrum would never be strong again, Mary recognized that his only chance to get well was for her to nurse him back to health. "I loved him so much that I felt if I could only care for him even for a few years it would be worth it," she said.[1]

That winter in Garden City, Utah, was a harsh one. Relatives in Ashley Valley, Uinta County, Utah, encouraged Hyrum and Mary to move near them, as the climate there was conducive to

Hyrum's regaining his full health and strength. The couple determined to move. They bought an eighty-acre farm which had on it a one-room log cabin, where their first child was born. Mary remembered, "When I heard his lusty cry I can truly say I had never before been so happy. Yes, lying there on a quilt on the little old cabin's floor with the man I loved so well and his dear old mother and sweet sisters around me, I know no one could be any more happy than I was."[2]

Mary bore nine children over the course of two decades. One son, Joseph Arthur, age three years, became very ill during the summer months of 1888. The family had planned to make the long journey to Logan, Utah, to be sealed in the Logan Temple that fall,

but the young boy's health grew worse to the point that they feared he would not survive the trip. Mary recalled, "We felt if we could get him to the Temple he would get well."[3] On October 12, 1888, Mary and Hyrum received their endowment in the Logan Temple, and the family was sealed. Little Arthur's grandmother worried that he would not live through the day, but Mary recorded that "the sisters took him and washed him and blessed him and he seemed much better."[4] With gratitude and renewed faith, the family journeyed home.

In 1890 the family moved to Wyoming to begin ranching. During the summer of 1894, Mary "felt a haunting fear that something awful was going to happen."[5] Arthur had been promised that in August, as soon as the haying was complete for the season, the family would travel to his grandmother's home near Bear Lake for Arthur's baptism before he turned nine in November. Mary recalled that Arthur was so excited to be baptized that he would awaken his father each morning and say, "Come, dadie, let's get the haying done so we can go to grand-ma's."[6] In August, Arthur's hard work and diligence was rewarded, and he was baptized in Bear Lake.

But tragedy struck just a short time later when Arthur drowned in a creek near their home in Wyoming. "It was a sad winter for me," Mary grieved. "I could not shed a tear at first, and after a while I would cry all the time when I was alone and at night when everyone else was asleep."[7]

One night Mary went to bed in despair, thinking that her situation could not have been worse, no matter how hard it had been in the past. When she finally fell asleep, she had a vivid dream in which she saw Arthur. "He looked very sad and there [were] tears in his big blue eyes," she recalled. "His lips quivered, and he said, 'I would be happy if my mamma did not cry so much.' That dream also was so real that it made me feel that I was making my loved one sad by grieving so."[8]

"I tried my best to get over my grieving and to once again be able to pray," Mary confessed. "It was a hard struggle."[9] Her decision to move forward amidst loss was a defining moment in Mary's life. She knew she had to rely on her faith and put her trust in the Lord, and she did. Although there continued to be times when she despaired, Mary was quick to recognize the Lord's hand in her life. When her beloved husband was later taken ill with pneumonia and passed away January 9, 1910, she faced the trial with courage.

"The rest of the winter was a very sad and lonely one," Mary commented, but she elected to live in hope. "I took up the burden of life again and worked harder than ever," Mary wrote. "I knew I had a big job to do if I kept my family together and raised them as I should."[10]

Mary's commitment to her faith found expression through years of service in her ward Young Ladies' Mutual Improvement Association and Relief Society and in the Logan Temple. Although she had little in the way of earthly goods, her door was always open. She and her family participated in many community activities, especially local theater and musical events. Mary spent her later years as a nurse, caring for her family and others through childbirth, recurrent illness, poverty, hunger, and death. And she consistently showed undaunted faith in the Lord and unwavering courage in the face of adversity.

From "It Would Be Worth It," by Jeff Hillam, in *Women of Faith in the Latter Days, Volume Three, 1846–1870*, edited by Richard E. Turley Jr. and Brittany A. Chapman (Salt Lake City: Deseret Book, 2014), 96–106.

An Enduring Faith

MARY GOBLE PAY

Mary Goble celebrated her thirteenth birthday shortly before her parents and five younger siblings arrived in America from Liverpool, England. Less than two weeks after joining the Saints who had gathered in Iowa City, Iowa, to prepare for their trek across the plains, Mary's youngest sister, Fanny, who had contracted measles on the ship, suffered from exposure during a severe thunderstorm and died just four days before her second birthday. Heartbroken but determined, the family began their journey to the Salt Lake Valley on September 1, 1856, with the Hunt wagon company. The company had been instructed to follow close behind the members of the Martin handcart company and stay near them to give support should they need help.

Mary's sister Edith was born in Nebraska a few weeks before the first major snowstorm of winter hit October 19, 1856. The emigrants had reached Wyoming by the time the snow came. Mary recalled:

"We traveled on till we got to the last crossing of the Platte River. That was the last walk I ever walked with my mother. We caught up with the handcart companies that day. We watched them cross the river. There were great lumps of ice floating down the river. It was bitter cold. The next morning there were 14 dead in their camp through the cold. We went back to camp went to prayers. They sang 'Come, come, ye Saints, no toil nor labor fear.' I wondered what made my mother cry."[1]

Conditions for the weary pioneers became more desperate with every day that passed. The trail was deep with snow, food was in short supply, and the cattle were so weak that they could go no more than a few miles each day.

"We did not know what would become of us," Mary remembered, "when one night a man came to our camp telling us there would be plenty of flour in the morning, for Bro. Brigham had sent men and teams to help us. There was rejoicing that night. Some sang, some danced, some cried. Well, he made a living Santy Claus. I have forgotten his name, but never will I forget how he looked. He was covered with the frost. His beard was long and all frost. His name was Eph Hanks."[2]

Nonetheless, Mary's suffering was not yet over. On November 3, Edith, her six-week-old sister, died for "want of nourishment."[3] Tender-hearted Mary remembered: "She was buried by the roadside. I felt I could not leave her, for I had seen so many graves opened by the wolves, and the team had got quite away when my father came back for me. I said, Oh, I cannot leave her to be eaten by the wolves; it seems so terrible. But he talked to me, and we hurried on."[4]

"When we arrived at Devil's Gate, it was bitter cold. . . . While there, an ox fell on the ice, and the brethren killed it, and the beef was given out to the camp. We made soup of it. My brother James ate a hearty supper. Was as well as he ever was when he went to bed. In the morning he was dead."[5]

The Goble family reached the Salt Lake Valley nearly seven months after they left their homeland: "We arrived in Salt Lake City 9 o clock at night the 11 of Dec 1856, 3 out of the 4 [children] that was living frozen, my mother dead in the wagon," Mary wrote. "Bishop Hardy had us taken to a house in his ward, and the brethren and sisters fetched us plenty of food. We had to be careful and not eat too much as it might kill us as we were so hungry."[6]

"Early next morning Bro. Brigham Young and a doctor came. . . . When Brigham Young came in, he shook hands with all of us. When he saw our condition, our feet frozen and our mother dead, tears rolled down his cheeks.

"The doctor wanted to cut my feet off at the ankles. But Pres. Young said, No, just cut off the toes, and I promise you, you will never have to take them off any farther. The pieces of bone that must come out will work out through the skin themselves. The doctor amputated my toes using a saw and a butcher knife."[7]

"The sisters were dressing mother for her grave. My poor father walked in the room where mother was, then back to us. He could not shed a tear. When our feet were fixed, they packed us in to see our mother for the last time. Oh, how did we stand it. That afternoon she was buried."[8]

The trials of Mary's youth refined her spirit and strengthened her for the challenges that lay ahead. At age sixteen, Mary married thirty-seven-year-old widower Richard Pay, who had also been a member of the Hunt wagon company. His first wife, Sarah, and their baby daughter had died during the trek to Utah. Several months after arriving in the Salt Lake Valley, Richard settled in Nephi, Utah. He and Mary were married there on June 26, 1859.

"When I was married it was hard times," wrote Mary. "My husband bought a one-room adobe house. . . . We had a bedstead, 3 chairs, table, a box for our flour. Our bed tick we filled with straw. We had 2 sheets, 2 pillow slips, one quilt. . . . We had 3 tin plates, 3 cups, a pan or two, a pot to cook in, and a spider to bake our bread in."[9]

Mary and Richard had thirteen children, four of whom died

before reaching adulthood. Seven were still at home in 1893 when, after returning from a journey to the Manti Temple, Richard suddenly became ill and died only a few days later. Mary was devastated by his death. With little means of support, she struggled to understand how she could raise a large family alone.

Mary wrote: "At the time . . . my husband died . . . I was left with 9 children [2 married]. I couldn't see wherein the Lord was justified in taking my husband and leaving me with so many mouths to feed and hardly any means of support. It didn't just seem right. I became almost bitter. And when neighbors kept saying, 'It was the will of the Lord that my husband was taken,' I felt that I could bear it no longer and told one to 'Shut up. I didn't want to hear that again.' The bishop and his counselors came to see me and said, 'It was the Lord's will.' I was so angry, I grabbed the broom and chased them from my yard. I was bitter toward the church—my neighbors, the Lord, even to staying away from church. And then one night I was lying not asleep but pondering—when my husband stood beside me, and he and I talked face to face. He told me that it was the Lord's will that he had been taken and that he was building a home for us in heaven and would not come back on earth if he could. He told me not to worry, that he would always be with me, and that soon Edward and Jesse [their sons] would secure work and would support the family. . . . He left me then, and the bitterness left my heart. I began to attend church. I loved my neighbor and asked the Lord's forgiveness for ever doubting His wisdom—soon my boys were working and supporting me and my family."[10]

In her patriarchal blessing, given in 1895, Mary was told, "Angels shall minister unto you and your husband also shall visit you in your night visions and dreams and comfort your heart as he is laboring in the ministry in the spirit world. . . . Therefore be patient in your trials and afflictions and no good thing shall be withheld from you."[11]

In the ensuing years, Mary told her children of several more visits her husband made to her in dreams, detailing the progress on their "house" in heaven. Phillip LeRoy Pay recorded: "I was the youngest child, . . . and about two years after I was married my mother took sick. She was living with my sister, Etta [Marietta Bowers], at the time. One morning she called my sister and said, 'Last night your father came to me and took me and showed me the house. It is all finished with furniture and everything. My, it is

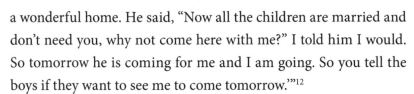

a wonderful home. He said, "Now all the children are married and don't need you, why not come here with me?" I told him I would. So tomorrow he is coming for me and I am going. So you tell the boys if they want to see me to come tomorrow.'"[12]

"My sister tried to talk her out of it by saying she was just dreaming. But Mother insisted she had not been asleep and was wide awake all the time, and she wanted all her boys called and to be there before 10 AM. My sister contacted all our family, and when we all arrived, Mother told us the above incident—and that she was going with our father to live with him. . . . She wanted us to know that she and our father would be waiting for us, and she wanted us to live clean lives and obey the commandments of the Lord so we could come and all live together again, and that she wanted us all to come. Then her happiness would be complete—but if we didn't all come, she would be filled with sorrow.

"Then just a few minutes before 10 AM she looked about—smiled a beautiful smile—gave a sigh and passed on. It was September 25, 1913."[13]

From "Angels Shall Minister unto You," by Christine Banks Bowers, Virginia H. Pearce, and Patricia H. Stoker, in *Women of Faith in the Latter Days, Volume Two, 1821–1845*, edited by Richard E. Turley Jr. and Brittany A. Chapman (Salt Lake City: Deseret Book, 2012), 243–57.

Faith Conquers Fear

DIANTHA MORLEY BILLINGS

Diantha Morley was just shy of her twentieth birthday when she first set foot on Ohio sod with her family. Near the rural village of Kirtland, Ohio, Diantha met and married Titus Billings, and they became members of Sidney Rigdon's Reformed Baptist congregation. In November 1830, Diantha and Titus, with Diantha's brother Isaac and his wife, Lucy, became Mormons.[1] Diantha is said to have been the first woman baptized in the Kirtland area, and many others from Rigdon's congregation followed.[2] At the time of her baptism, Diantha had five living children under the age of twelve, and she had buried three others as infants.

Diantha and Isaac were the only members of the larger Morley family to join the Church in Kirtland. Estranged from their parents for doing so, Diantha and Isaac forged a strong bond and remained close throughout the rest of their lives. Diantha's husband was a sometime business partner with Isaac, and the two families spent most of the next thirty years living near each other.

Diantha and her family, along with the rest of the Saints, faced many challenging circumstances, and she became known for her ability to maintain her composure and take charge of a situation, refusing to allow fear to get in the way of action. One incident that happened during the 1833 persecution of the Saints in Missouri, Diantha's daughter Eunice remembered, was "the burning of Uncle Isaac Morley's cooper shop. It was full of cooper wooden ware, such as barrels, tubs, churns, and numerous other articles he had made to sell. The mob set it on fire." The next night, Diantha and her children "were ordered to leave our home or we would be served the same way."

Since Titus was away, Diantha and "some fifteen or twenty of the sisters got together and counseled what to do. They decided to take their smallest children and flee to a house out of town a short distance. . . . We had to go about three-quarters of a mile in the dark, and there were no two women allowed to go together" to minimize the risk of being seen by the mob. "My mother had three of her children with her and not one of us had one bite of supper. In going to that place, Mother took her children and went through the fields, through briers and all kinds of stubble. She carried a lantern half concealed under her apron. I, being the youngest of the three children, held on to her skirts while she led the way.

"We had to cross the main road at a point where four other roads crossed and where some very large trees stood. As mother stepped into the road a man came from behind one of the trees and flashed a bright sword in her face. She jumped back and screamed. The man soon made himself known. He was one of the brethren guarding the cross roads. . . . Mother said if ever she was glad to meet a friend it was at that time."[3] The women arrived safely with their children and began putting them to bed.

"I remember well how my limbs were scratched and how they bled when I was put to bed," Diantha's daughter Eunice recalled, "and I was not allowed to cry or make a loud noise. The room where we slept was a large log room. The floor was completely covered with children and some of them did not even have a quilt over or under them."[4]

Five years later, Diantha and her family were living in Far West, Missouri, when her husband was involved in the Battle of Crooked River between the Mormons and the Missourians. David Patten, an apostle and the commander of the militia in which Titus served, was killed, and the Latter-day Saint men in the battle had to flee the state for safety. Their families fended for themselves while the city of Far West lay under siege.

Diantha had children to care for and was also a midwife and nurse. In the midst of the siege, Diantha was called to the bedside of Eliza Ann Carter Snow, who recorded: "We went to Missouri . . . and there my first child was born: it was the 30th day of October in the year 1838. . . . It was cold and snowed every day and the mob came into Far West the very day of her birth, and we were much excited. I could not keep the midwife long enough to dress my child, Sister Diantha Billings was her name, well known among our people. The mob was blowing horns and firing guns all night long. We were without bread or anything to make bread of, but by the help of the Lord we were preserved."[5] Both Eliza and her daughter, Sarah Jane, survived that eventful night, due in part to Diantha's good care and her ability to stay calm in the face of danger.

Diantha's services as a nurse and midwife continued to be in demand when the family moved to Illinois, where her regular patients included the Prophet Joseph Smith's family. During this time, her youngest son, ten-year-old Titus, died of a brain inflammation, despite everything that could be done for him. Diantha was certainly no stranger to such profound loss: Titus was the fourth child she had buried. Within the next few years her two older sons, Samuel and Ebenezer, left the Church and the family. Diantha never saw them again, but her faith and courage did not waver.

After the exodus from Nauvoo, the Billings family spent the winter of 1846–47 some distance outside Winter Quarters at a Ponca Indian camp, where they "were uniformly used well by the Indians, had good forage for the cattle, etc."[6] Diantha's daughter Eunice remembered: "One beautiful night the prairie became suddenly ablaze with fire, from some cause, we knew not what, and the flames were rushing directly for our haystacks, which were in a straight path for them. In case the stack caught, our fortification would surely go, when through the mercy of the Lord, the wind died down and the fire subsided, leaving us safe, and our hay stacks unharmed. Kegs of powder and other inflammable material in the camp were pitched into a stream called Running Water, in order to protect the travelers that night from the fury of a prairie fire. . . . It is needless to say that the women and children were frightened and had it not been for my mother, who was acting as a nurse, some of the women would have committed themselves to the rushing waters when the fire raged on the prairie."[7]

The Billings family started the trek west from Winter Quarters in the spring of 1848. Diantha served as a midwife as the Saints journeyed across the plains of Iowa and on to the Salt Lake Valley. The trail record kept by Thomas Bullock notes that "Huldah Mariah Ballantyne Wife of Richard Ballantyne was safely delivered of a boy."[8] Because the child was sickly, it was feared he would not survive. But he and his mother did pull through.

That was not the case, however, with all of Diantha's patients. After her family was called to settle in what is now the Sanpete Valley of central Utah, Diantha's first patient was her own daughter Eunice, who was expecting her first child—Diantha's first grandchild. Eunice recalled that "due to hardship and suffering the little thing was still-born, and I came very nearly to losing my own life. I was sick for quite a while, and my mother, who was a midwife, nursed and attended me. She was the only doctor, midwife, and nurse at the time in Manti."[9]

Once again, Diantha had been unable to save a beloved family member, but she continued to serve as a nurse and midwife for as long as her health allowed. She was described by Emmeline B. Wells as one of the "noble mothers in Israel with kindly deeds and loving words [who] inspired many a fainting heart with faith and courage and ministered temporal and spiritual blessings to hundreds of the daughters of Zion, whose paths were not strewn with roses, but were full of thorns and fiery trials and needed their encouragement."[10]

From "Rejoice Notwithstanding the Trials," by Catherine Wheelwright Ockey, in *Women of Faith in the Latter Days, Volume One, 1775–1820,* edited by Richard E. Turley Jr. and Brittany A. Chapman (Salt Lake City: Deseret Book, 2011), eBook.

Rich in Character

ELIZABETH ANN CLARIDGE McCUNE

Elizabeth Ann Claridge spent the years of her childhood on the edge of civilization. Born in England in 1852, shortly after her parents joined the Church, Elizabeth was a baby when her parents crossed the Atlantic and migrated to Salt Lake City. They were asked to continue on to a new settlement called Salt Creek, eighty-nine miles to the south. So it was that in April of 1854, two-year-old Elizabeth arrived with her parents at Salt Creek (later renamed Nephi), the small frontier town she would ever after think of as home.

Elizabeth worked hard with her family to eke out an existence and garner a few hard-earned luxuries. "There was no place on earth that was so precious to me as dear old Nephi," Elizabeth recalled later in life. "We were happy—perfectly so, and as proud of our station and of the parts we played as a people could be."[1]

The fact that everyone was poor didn't keep them from enjoying life. "We proved in those days that it is not necessary to be rich to be happy," she observed. "Nephi was not large, not wonderful, but we had our occasions there, as we called them, just as much so as any big city of the land. And what is more, we got out of them every ounce of pleasure they would yield."[2]

Perhaps the most memorable of those occasions for Elizabeth was an 1867 visit by President Brigham Young. Accompanied by a party of Church authorities, he was welcomed by Elizabeth's family and others who had done their best to make things look stylish for their distinguished guests from the city. Wearing new white dresses, fifteen-year-old Elizabeth and her friends were seated in the front for the afternoon meeting. Toward the close of the meeting, President Young announced that some of the men would be called to go with their families and "settle the Muddy," a new settlement along the Muddy River near present-day Logandale in the bleak desert of southern Nevada.

Elizabeth's heart nearly stopped. Some members of their community had previously been called to settle the Dixie country in southern Utah, but the Muddy was much farther away and a much more barren and difficult land to tame. "Then I heard the name of 'Samuel Claridge,' my father. After that I knew nothing for a moment and when I recovered myself again I was weeping bitterly. Tears were spoiling my new white dress but I sobbed on just the same."[3]

Elizabeth's friend seated next to her whispered, "What are you feeling so badly about? My father has been called, too, but you see that I am not crying because I know he won't go."[4]

"That is just the difference," Elizabeth replied through her tears. "My father is called and I know that he WILL GO; and that nothing can prevent him from going. He never fails to do anything when called upon; and badly as I feel about it I would be ashamed if he didn't go."[5]

Elizabeth journeyed to the Muddy with her father and his second wife, reluctantly leaving behind her friends, mother and sister, and the comfortable childhood home that was so dear to her. But inspired by her father's insistence on answering the call to "build up another waste place in Zion," Elizabeth labored vigorously to help construct a new home and make a life for her family in the desert.[6]

"My father built a house away down on the Muddy," Elizabeth later wrote. "I helped my father build it. I worked just as hard as a man. Every adobe and every bucket of mortar that went into its walls I carried. Yes, every one. It was a hard task but I am not ashamed of it and would do it again under like circumstances if it were necessary. My father was a good man and I was proud of the fact that I was able to lighten his burden in some measure."[7]

For three years Elizabeth worked side by side with her father to settle the Muddy, until the Muddy Mission was abandoned in 1870 and Elizabeth moved to St. George to work in the telegraph office.[8] Her attitude toward work, wealth, and worldly attainments was forged by these pioneering experiences and remained with her throughout her life. When she later married Alfred William McCune and later still moved to Salt Lake City, her husband's mining and timber interests became the beginning of spectacular business successes that catapulted the family into prominence as one of Utah's wealthiest families.

The contrast between her pioneer upbringing and her new situation could not have been greater, yet Elizabeth maintained her

unpretentious character. She made regular generous donations to a variety of causes and individuals and avoided hiring servants. Her hesitance to indulge in extravagance prompted her husband to say that "the greatest fault he could find with her was that she would not spend freely enough what he so lavishly bestowed upon her."[9]

Eventually Elizabeth and her husband, Alfred, built a home at 200 North

Main Street in Salt Lake City. Considered by many to be the finest in Utah, the residence served as the family home for nearly two decades. But because Alfred's business ventures kept him frequently on the road, and as their seven surviving children (Elizabeth gave birth to nine) began to leave home, Elizabeth grew lonely in the enormous mansion. In 1920, the couple donated the home to the Church to be used for whatever purpose the First Presidency deemed best.

After considering various possibilities, Church leaders decided to convert the home, known today as the McCune Mansion, into a Church-operated school. After Elizabeth's death, the school was named the McCune School of Music and Art, and the building served educational purposes in the Church for nearly forty years.

From "Doing a Little Good for the Cause of Christ," by Matthew S. McBride, in *Women of Faith in the Latter Days, Volume Three, 1846–1870,* edited by Richard E. Turley Jr. and Brittany A. Chapman (Salt Lake City: Deseret Book, 2014), 107–21.

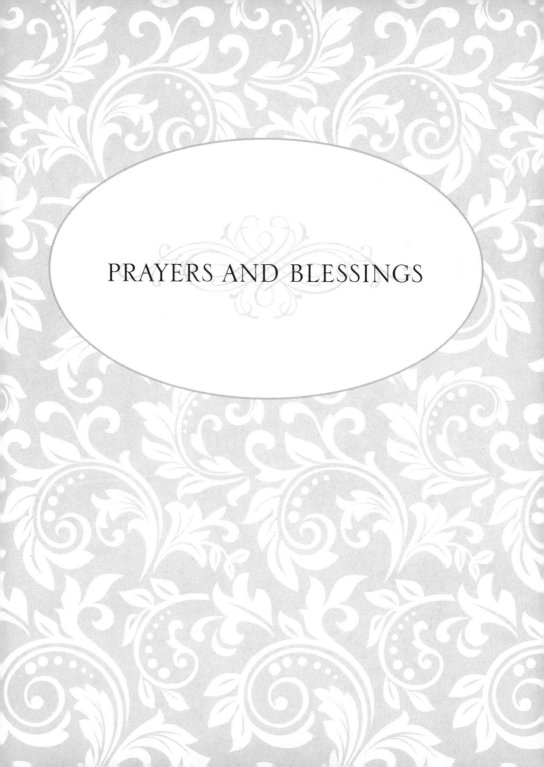

PRAYERS AND BLESSINGS

A Blessing and a Call

SARAH LOUISA YATES ROBISON

Born in a log house in Scipio, Utah, in 1866, Sarah Louisa Yates experienced a typical pioneering childhood. Though means were scarce, Louise (as she preferred to be known) was fortunate to attend a "better than the average pioneer school" in Scipio, followed by a year at Brigham Young Academy in Provo and six months' training as a dressmaker in Salt Lake City.[1]

After she married Joseph Lyman Robison in 1883, the couple lived in Fillmore for six years before moving to Provo. There Louise noticed a sore on her face that was eventually diagnosed as cancer. She sought treatment and a blessing. Her bishop sent for the stake patriarch, Pat Blackburn, who gave her a patriarchal blessing before administering to her. "God healed me," Louise testified. "Brother Blackburn told me in my blessing that my voice [would] be heard in many parts of the world, but until I moved to Provo, I had not held an office in the Church. There I was secretary of the Mutual [now called Young Women]."[2]

Her face healed without scarring or the need for surgery, and the patriarch's blessing was fulfilled through the service she gave over the remainder of her life.

From Provo, the family moved first to Logan and then to Salt Lake City. Louise continued to serve in her ward and community, particularly with the Red Cross during World War I. For this service, she received the Red Cross pin, a recognition that meant much to her. In 1914, Louise was called to serve in the Salt Lake Granite Stake Relief Society, first as a board member and then as a counselor in the stake Relief Society presidency.

One of Louise's maxims was "Welcome the task that takes you beyond yourself,"[3] and she would often "volunteer for the hardest, grubbiest work."[4] Her daughter Gladys described seeing Louise "in the middle of mounds of old clothes and old shoes sorting, sorting and matching pairs, and selecting and packing piles of clothing to be sent to . . . unfortunate refugees."[5]

In the spring of 1921, Louise attended the Relief Society general conference with her sister Lizzie Thompson. "It had been announced that there would be a re-organization of the Relief Society General Board," Louise's daughter Gladys related, "so when President [Heber J.] Grant released Emmeline B. Wells, and presented the name of Clarissa S. Williams as General President, Mother was delighted to give her a sustaining vote, as she had worked with Sister Williams and knew her to be a fine, capable woman."

When President Grant announced the names of Jennie Knight and Louise Robison as Sister Williams's counselors and asked for a sustaining vote, Louise raised her hand in approval. She "turned to her sister and said, 'I didn't know there was another woman working in the Relief Society who had a name so much like mine!' Her sister answered, 'Why, Louie, that's you! You have just sustained yourself!' Mother nearly fainted."[6]

Louise's experience at the conference not only reflects how Church callings were often issued at the time but also speaks volumes about her unassuming nature. For several days she agonized about the call, concerned that she was not someone the women of the Church would look up to. Feeling certain that President Grant had been misinformed about her abilities, she summoned the courage to voice her fears to the prophet when she went to his office to be set apart.

Louise's daughter Gladys wrote that her mother told President Grant "she'd be happy to do her best in whatever he asked her to do, but she wanted him to know that she had a limited education, and very little money and social position, and she was afraid she wouldn't be the example that the women of the Relief Society would expect in a leader. She finished by saying, 'I'm just a humble woman!' President Grant answered, 'Sister Louisy, 85% of the women of our Church are humble women. We are calling you to be the leader of them.'"[7]

It was the beginning of a new era in Louise's life. Her daughter later recalled, "Mother never forgot what she felt was a special call, and through her administration, her main concern was for those who were underprivileged because of lack of money or opportunity for education."[8]

Seven years later, on the eve of the Great Depression, Louisa Yates Robison was called to be the seventh general president of the

Relief Society. Sustained on October 7, 1928, she served for eleven turbulent years. Lack of employment was rampant throughout the United States at this time, and Utah was no exception. Louise reminded the sisters that the purpose of Relief Society was to reach out to individual sisters with support and assistance. "This is the first requirement of our Relief Society," she instructed. "Never become blind to the needs of the poor or deaf to their cries."[9] Throughout her service, she maintained direct supervision over the Welfare Department of the Relief Society. She worked with public health nurses, the state board of health, and other agencies in providing support and assistance to bishops in the Salt Lake Valley.

Among her many contributions was the establishment of Mormon Handicraft in 1937. The economic effects of the Great Depression forced many women to work outside the home to help support their families, but Louise felt strongly that wherever possible, mothers of small children should be in the home rather than in the workplace. Mormon Handicraft was conceived as an outlet for women to market their home crafts.

In her patriarchal blessing, Louise had been told her voice would be heard in many parts of the world. In 1929 she became the first general Relief Society president to address the Church in general conference, speaking with an impromptu invitation. As she stood before the Church, she began, "My brethren and sisters, I am sure you will know that I need your faith and prayers, but I do love to bear my testimony."[10]

Louise was the first general Relief Society president to visit branches and districts of the Church in England and Europe. As general president of the Relief Society, she was a participating member of the National Council of Women and attended national and international conferences. In 1934, she traveled to Paris for an International Council of Women conference as one of only nine American women chosen to be delegates.

Louise proved to be a woman well suited for her time. Aware of her own limited education and means, she reached out to others who struggled in similar circumstances. Although she was described as "the shyest and most self-effacing of women," this humble woman overcame her timid nature and feelings of inadequacy to lead the Relief Society through an era of severe economic challenges.[11] Her theme became, "Go where you're needed; do what you can," a standard still relevant today.[12]

From "Welcome the Task That Takes You beyond Yourself," by Patricia Lemmon Spilsbury, in *Women of Faith in the Latter Days, Volume Three, 1846–1870,* edited by Richard E. Turley Jr. and Brittany A. Chapman (Salt Lake City: Deseret Book, 2014), 146–57.

Mill Stone believed to be from Haun's Mill (1836 - CA 1845).
This relic represents a tragic episode in American religious
history. A testament to an enduring need for greater
understanding and tolerance between peoples of differing
ideologies, including religious beliefs and cultural backgounds.

As a result of miscommunication and feelings of powerlessness
to effect change in the wake of what they saw as
offensive Mormon military actions in Daviess County,
Livingston County Regulators and other volunteers, brutally attacked
the nearby Mormon settlement of Haun's Mill, on Shoal Creek,
30 October 1838, killing 17 persons, 14 of whom were hastily
interred in a partially completed well on the site.

In memory of the massacre, local residents moved
this Mill Stone to Breckenridge sometime after 1927.

Dedicated May 26, 2001
City of Breckenridge Park Board
& Missouri Mormon Frontier Foundation

"I Knew Not What to Do"

AMANDA BARNES SMITH

The life story of Amanda Barnes Smith is a testament to the remarkable power of God helping us in our darkest hours.

In 1826, Amanda married Warren Smith, a man fifteen years her senior who had been in love with another woman. Warren told her, "I love you, but I love her little finger more than I love your whole body."[1] Despite his divided affection, Warren was a good provider, and Amanda wrote, "We had plenty of this world's goods and lived co[m]fortable and happily together."[2]

They accepted the restored gospel in 1831, and after experiencing devastating financial losses in Kirtland, Ohio, outfitted a team, loaded their remaining household possessions, and prepared to journey with their five children to join the Saints living in Caldwell County, Missouri. Before leaving, they stopped in Amherst to bid farewell to their family and former neighbors. "The treatment that we received will never be forgot[t]en by me," Amanda wrote. "My mother said she hoped she would never see me hear of me nor hear my name mentioned again. But we bid them good by[e] and left them."[3] Her mother's desires were fulfilled. Amanda never saw her parents nor any of her siblings again.

Unaware of the turmoil in Caldwell County, Missouri, between local citizens and the members of the Church, the Smith family stopped at a small Latter-day Saint settlement called Hawn's Mill to rest for a few days.

Amanda vividly described the scene: "A little before sunset a mob of three hundred armed men came upon us. Our brethren shouted for the women and children to run for the woods, while they (the men) ran into an old blacksmith shop.

"They feared, if men, women and children were in one place, the mob would rush upon them and kill them all together. The mob fired before the women had time to start from the camp. The men took off their hats and swung them and cried for quarter, until they were shot down; the mob paid no attention to their cries nor their entreaties but fired alternately."[4]

As the mob fired, Amanda and her little girls ran for the woods (she could not find her boys). "The bullets whistled by me like hailstones, and cut down the bushes on all sides," she recalled. "I witnessed that awful scene, which can never, no never, be erased from my memory while I live upon the earth; I can shut my eyes at any time and see it all over again. The shock to my nervous system no language can define."[5]

The mob drove away with the settlers' horses and wagons, leaving behind a scene of slaughter and destruction. "The groans of the wounded and dying rent the air," Amanda remembered, as the women and children made their way back to the settlement.[6] She found her husband and ten-year-old son lifeless on the ground. Her six-year-old son, Alma, lay wounded and bleeding.

"The entire hip joint of my wounded boy had been shot away," Amanda recorded. "Flesh, hip bone, joint and all had been ploughed out from the muzzle of the gun which the ruffian placed to the child's hip through the logs of the shop and deliberately fired. We laid little Alma on a bed in our tent and I examined the wound. It was a ghastly sight. I knew not what to do. It was night now. . . .

"Oh my Heavenly Father, I cried, what shall I do? Thou seest my poor wounded boy and knowest my inexperience. Oh Heavenly Father direct me what to do!

"And then I was directed as by a voice speaking to me.

"The ashes of our fire was still smouldering. . . . I was directed to take those ashes and make a lye and put a cloth saturated with it right into the wound. It hurt, but little Alma was too near dead to heed it much. Again and again I saturated the cloth and put it into the hole from which the hip-joint had been ploughed. . . .

"Having done as directed I again prayed to the Lord and was again instructed as distinctly as though a physician had been standing by speaking to me.

"Near by was a slippery-elm tree. From this I was told to make a slippery-elm poultice and fill the wound with it. My eldest boy was sent to get the slippery-elm from the roots, the poultice was made; and the wound, which took fully a quarter of a yard of linen to cover, so large was it, was properly dressed.

"It was then I found vent to my feelings in tears, and resigned myself to the anguish of the hour. . . .

"I removed the wounded boy to a house, some distance off, the next day, and dressed his hip; the Lord directing me as before. I was reminded that in my husband's trunk there was a bottle of balsam. This I poured into the wound, greatly soothing Alma's pain.

"'Alma, my child,' I said, 'you believe that the Lord made your hip?'

"'Yes, Mother.'

"'Well, the Lord can make something there in the place of your hip, don't you believe he can, Alma?'

"'Do you think that the Lord can, mother?' inquired the child, in his simplicity.

"'Yes, my son,' I replied, 'he has shown it all to me in a vision.'

"Then I laid him comfortably on his face, and said: 'Now you lay like that, and don't move, and the Lord will make you another hip.'

"So Alma laid on his face for five weeks, until he was entirely recovered—a flexible gristle having grown in place of the missing joint and socket," which was "a marvel to physicians."[7]

While Alma was healing, the marauders continued to oppress Mormon families living near the mill. Like Amulon in the Book of Mormon, who forbade the followers of Alma to pray, during this time the vigilantes threatened to kill the Mormon survivors if they did not stop praying.[8] Amanda yearned to pray vocally for some respite from her distress. "I could bear it no longer," she wrote, and, in the midst of her sorrow, she found seclusion in a cornfield.[9] There she poured out her heart and soul to God. As she emerged from the corn, she heard a voice repeat a verse from the hymn "How Firm a Foundation":

That soul who on Jesus hath leaned for repose,
I cannot, I will not desert to its foes:
That soul, though all hell should endeavor to shake,
I'll never, no never, no never forsake![10]

From that moment on, she had no fear for herself or her children.

Like most of the Saints, Amanda and her four surviving children made their way out of Missouri in the middle of winter, first to Quincy, Illinois, and later to Nauvoo. She supported her family by teaching school. When the Saints met more persecution in Nauvoo and were again driven from their homes, Amanda's faith did not waver. She and her children journeyed to join with the main body of the Church in the Salt Lake Valley.

The testimony she bore still resonates today: "I have drunk the bitter dregs of the cup of sorrow and affliction, as well as partaken of the blessing of an all merciful God. . . . I have seen the Lord's power manifest to a great degree. I have seen the lame leap as an hart [a male deer], the eyes of the blind open, and as it were, the dead raised to life—all in my own family since I have been a member of the Church of Jesus Christ. . . . I feel that of all women I have the greatest reason to rejoice and thank my Heavenly Father; and I do thank and praise his holy name for his blessings to me; and I do desire that I may ever be kept faithful unto the end that I may receive the reward of the just."[11]

From "I'll Never Forsake," by Alexander L. Baugh, in *Women of Faith in the Latter Days, Volume One, 1775–1820*, edited by Richard E. Turley Jr. and Brittany A. Chapman (Salt Lake City: Deseret Book, 2011), 327–42.

"I Prayed for Him in Secret"

LUCY HANNAH WHITE FLAKE

Lucy Hannah White was born to parents who had joined with the Saints and later settled in Nauvoo, where they provided a strong, religious home that became the foundation of Lucy's life. Her family, one of the last to leave that beautiful city, spent three years in Winter Quarters. Lucy was eight years old when she and her family crossed the plains in 1850. Eventually they settled in Cedar City, in southern Utah, where she met her future husband, William Flake, whom Lucy described as "tall and well built; . . . well mannered and chivalrous." The young couple was married by Elder Amasa Lyman of the Quorum of the Twelve and began their life together in Beaver, fifty miles north of Cedar City. The newlyweds had very little to establish their home, but they were not far from Lucy's parents, and they were happy and thankful for what they did have. "We loved each other and loved our home," she later recalled.[1]

As was true of many women on the western frontier, Lucy had not received much formal schooling, but, her daughter Lucy wrote, she "was a schoolteacher before she was married." She later taught her children their "letters out of the Bible as [we] had no schoolbook."[2]

William supported his family largely by freighting, farming, and raising livestock, which gave Lucy additional responsibilities when he was on the road between Salt Lake and California. She began one diary entry by listing her typical morning chores, which included tending and feeding her chickens and the neighbor's, drawing water, putting potatoes on to cook, brushing and sweeping half an inch of dust off the floor, and making breakfast. That particular morning she also "had to go half [a] mile after calves." She concluded philosophically, "This is the way of life on the farm."[3]

And there were other challenges. Early in their marriage, Lucy confided in her journal that her husband was not religious. Although she encouraged family prayer, William declined to participate. "This was somewhat of a trial to me," she wrote, "but I loved him and prayed for him in secret." Still, William did not respond to Lucy's pleadings, telling her that "he was going to be religious when he got old."[4]

Perhaps as a compromise, just before a long freighting trip, William finally promised he would pray with Lucy "if he ever got home again." Three months passed before he returned from the arduous trip. Lucy reminded him of his promise. That night, William knelt and gave the first prayer she had ever heard him utter. From that time forward, he knelt in prayer with his family every evening.

In 1861, Lucy's second son, two-month-old William Melvin, passed away. "I can say his death was the first trial of my faith," Lucy wrote. "It seemed my prayers had always been answered before, but in his sickness it seemed like my prayers did no good but still I kept trying to get my Heavenly Father to hear me. Kept praying but it seemed he could not hear me."[5]

After the death of her child, Lucy's yearning to receive temple blessings intensified. She wanted to have her family sealed eternally. During William's long absences on freighting trips, Lucy felt unsettled. "I was lonely and had plenty of time to pray as I was anxious for my husband's welfare," she wrote. She pleaded with the Lord "for the time to come for us to be worthy to go and get our endowments."[6]

During one of William's trips, Lucy wrote to her husband and asked him to meet her in Salt Lake City for the upcoming October general conference. He did so, and they attended the sessions together. Then, at the conclusion of the conference, the bishop of

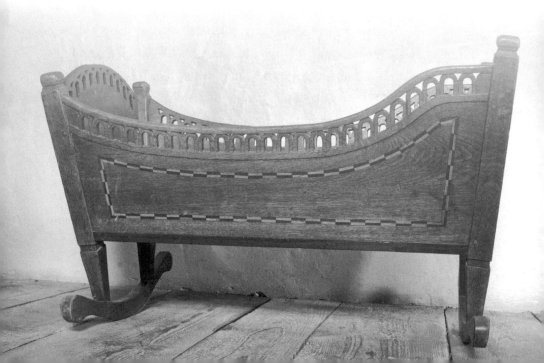

their ward spoke to William. He said, "Brother William, I want you and your wife to come to the Endowment House." William was so surprised he didn't know what to say. Lucy recalled that "if the bishop had told him he wanted him to go to England he could not [have] felt more surprised. He tried to get excused, saying he did not think himself worthy," she wrote, "but the bishop would not let him off. . . . That night I was so thankful [I] hardly slept." On October 9, 1861, Lucy rejoiced, "we received that great blessing and were sealed for time and all eternity."[7]

Years later, President Brigham Young called the family to settle a new community in Arizona. "Sell all that you have, that you can't take with you," he instructed William. "Take your family and go there [Arizona] to settle the Saints. Leave nothing to come back to."[8] William "felt dreadful bad," recalled Lucy, "but we were called and there was no other way."[9]

The move was extremely difficult for Lucy and her family. Conditions were primitive at best, and the harsh environment bred illness. Her youngest child, George, became sick. "I did all I could with medicine and also with faith," Lucy wrote. "On the morning of July 6th [18]78 I was so deep in sorrow it seemed I could not bear it any longer. I went out in some brush out of sight and asked my Father in Heaven to take him home for I could not bear it any longer. My burden was heavier than I could bear. That prayer was simple but from my heart. I went to him. He breathed a few times and passed away so sweetly."[10]

William searched for more suitable land for a settlement and found a site nestled in a little valley called Silver Creek. Lucy remembered, "This beautiful valley was a bit of Heaven reserved for

us as a reward for all we had suffered.
. . . I poured out my gratitude" in
prayer.[11] Lucy concluded in her
journal, "We have had many trials and sorrows but the Lord
has greatly blessed us."[12]

There William and Lucy established a township that was
renamed in honor of its founder,
William Jordan Flake, and
apostle Erastus Snow. Snowflake,
Arizona, became the Flakes' per-
manent home for the rest of their lives.
Of their thirteen children, only eight survived to
adulthood. But less than sixty years after her death, Lucy's posterity
exceeded seven thousand souls, and the town that bore her family's name eventually became the home of the Snowflake Arizona
Temple.

From "The Lord Has Greatly Blessed Us," by David F. Boone, in *Women of Faith in the Latter Days, Volume Two, 1821–1845,* edited by Richard E. Turley Jr. and Brittany A. Chapman (Salt Lake City: Deseret Book, 2012), 76–90.

The Lord Works in Mysterious Ways

SARAH ANN NELSON PETERSON

I n the Stavanger region of Norway's western coast in 1825, a group of devout Quakers seeking religious freedom embarked on the first organized emigration from Norway to America. The company purchased a sloop—a small sailing vessel just fifty-four feet long and sixteen feet wide that was better suited to coastal fishing than to trans-Atlantic voyages—and set off on the perilous journey with fifty-two people aboard, including Cornelius and Carrie Nelson. They settled in upstate New York, where the couple's daughter, Sarah Ann, was born in 1827, becoming—by her own account—the second Norwegian born in America.

Sarah moved in May 1836 with her widowed mother to a new settlement of Norwegian immigrants on the Fox River in LaSalle County, Illinois. There, in 1842, Sarah heard and embraced the restored gospel. A few years later, in the spring of 1849, twenty-two-year-old Sarah bade her family good-bye and, reminiscent of her parents' journey to seek religious freedom, joined a company of pioneers who were preparing to leave for the Salt Lake Valley. Sarah was not the only one to make the journey without family members. Twenty-five-year-old Canute Peterson, a friend of the family, was also part of that group of Norwegian converts seeking to gather with the Saints in Utah.

On their way to Council Bluffs, the company traveled about two hundred miles to Burlington, Iowa, and discovered that it was practically deserted on account of an epidemic of cholera, a leading cause of death on the overland trails in the mid-nineteenth century. The disease, caused by water-borne bacteria, was particularly virulent along transportation routes and resulted in death for half of all untreated victims. Symptoms of vomiting, acute diarrhea, dehydration, and severe intestinal cramping typically came on quickly, often running their course in a matter of hours until death came as a relief to its victims.

The group passed through the city as quickly as they could and camped about eight miles away on a little creek, but by the time they reached Chardon Point, Iowa, Sarah had been seized with a violent attack of the deadly disease. The women in the traveling party did all they could for her relief, but to no avail, and her death seemed imminent.

During Sarah's illness, Canute Peterson realized he loved the young woman he had known since his youth. He wrote: "I was impressed to go down into the woods on the creek and pray to the Lord for her recovery. Here I earnestly besought the Lord that He would spare her life," he recalled, "and I became so filled with the Spirit of the Lord that I thought I hardly touched the ground while going from the place of prayer to the wagon.

"When within a few rods of the wagon, I could hear her groan. I went to the side of the wagon nearest her head, put my hand between the wagon cover and the wagon box, and placed my hand on her head and silently rebuked the Destroyer.

"She immediately straightened herself out of the cramp, smiled, and told the Sisters, 'I am healed.'

"She was well aware whose hand it was that had touched her. She had the disease no more."[1]

As the company crossed Iowa, the two young people courted and decided to marry. Canute was twenty-five and had little to offer his bride other than a meager traveling outfit and "his honest heart," but that was enough for Sarah.[2] Soon after arriving at the Missouri River, the two were married by apostle Orson Hyde at a camp five miles east of Kanesville, Iowa. Two weeks later they set out for the West.

Dedicated to building both their family and the kingdom of God, the young couple survived other trials, including a four-year separation while Canute served a mission to Norway. Twenty-five years old and pregnant with their second child, Sarah bade her husband good-bye, knowing that she would now become the primary provider for their small family. She worked their farm in Lehi, some thirty miles south of Salt Lake City, gave birth to a baby girl, and endured uncertainty, tensions with native people, and famine. Drought, accompanied by infestations of crop-eating insects, devastated several harvests, but in 1855, three years after Canute departed on his mission, a few fields were spared, including Sarah's. Unable to obtain assistance with tilling the land, Sarah had "attempted the planting of the crop herself. In furrows made with a hoe, she planted the precious kernels of wheat and because of her anxiety to perform the work well, she covered them deeply with soil." It was grueling, back-breaking work and late in the season by the time she was finished. But "because of the lateness and depth of planting, [Sarah's] wheat did not show above the ground until after the 1855 grasshopper infestation had passed. When the other fields were barren and waste, that of Mrs. Peterson was covered with a luxuriant growth. Sixty bushels of wheat was the generous reward bestowed by Mother Earth, in addition to, sixty bushels of corn, and some potatoes."[3] During the following winter, Sarah was able to provide for her family, as well as seven orphans, and to give generous aid to numerous neighbors.

Returning home from his mission in 1856, Canute penned a letter to Sarah from Fort Laramie, Wyoming. He gave an account of the successful emigrating company he had arranged and issued her a good-natured challenge: "Now if you can beat that I think you have done well."[4] Arriving in Lehi, he was pleasantly surprised. Not only had Sarah sustained her little family and cared for others but her hard work had paid off, and they were "in a much better condition financially than when he left."[5]

The Petersons' farm continued to prosper, and the family was well-respected in the community. Their large home was open to the many Scandinavians traveling between Salt Lake City and the southern settlements. Sarah remained humble and grateful for the hand of the Lord in her life, remarking to a group of young women, "We do not all need the visiting of angels, but we should know within our own hearts that the gospel is true."[6]

From "We Are Blessed as Sisters," by Jennifer L. Lund, in *Women of Faith in the Latter Days, Volume Two, 1821–1845*, edited by Richard E. Turley Jr. and Brittany A. Chapman (Salt Lake City: Deseret Book, 2012), 258–74.

THE INFLUENCE OF
RIGHTEOUS WOMEN

"Of More Value Than Soles"

ANNA KARINE GAARDEN WIDTSOE

The tiny, remote island of Frøya, Norway, on the westernmost fragment of the Norwegian coast, fostered a rugged people who knew how to survive and to be resilient in the face of tragedy.

Anna Karine Gaarden was only twelve years old when her mother died, leaving her to run the household for her father and younger sister, Pertroline Jørgine. Anna had learned to read and write from her educated and prosperous parents and attended school whenever the traveling teacher visited their small village. It was a tender mercy that the year her mother died, a new school-teacher, John Anders Widtsoe, arrived in the community and, recognizing Anna's intelligence, began tutoring her privately. Mutual admiration grew, and six years later the couple became engaged. After John completed his university degree, the couple married.

On January 31, 1872, Anna and John were blessed with a son, whom they named John Andreas Widtsoe for his father. The family moved to the Norwegian mainland, where Osborne John Peter was born on December 12, 1877. But tragedy struck just two months after the birth of little Osborne, when Anna's husband died of a sudden illness in the dark depths of a Norwegian winter. The heartbroken twenty-eight-year-old widow, whose father had also died a few years before, felt lost and very alone. Standing by the grave, watching her little boy drop a crimson rose onto the casket, Anna received no hope of a future reunion from the priest's words "Dust thou art, to dust returnest."

Pained by lingering memories and driven by her resolve to educate her two sons and shape their lives as a legacy to her husband, Anna moved to Trondheim, the old capital city of Norway, where she felt the boys' opportunities for schooling would be improved. She established herself as a dressmaker and gradually auctioned off her husband's vast library to provide for her family. Providentially, she came into contact with some of her husband's friends, and at their urging the government gave her a small lifetime pension in recognition of her husband's service in education, including provision for her sons' own education. Their future seemed assured.[1]

In the spring of 1879, Anna sent a pair of young John's shoes to a shoemaker for repair. When the shoemaker's son delivered the mended shoes, Anna found some religious tracts tucked inside. When Anna returned to the shoemaker with another pair of shoes that needed repair, she asked him about the meaning of the tracts. The brave shoemaker said, "You may be surprised to hear me say that I can give you something of more value than soles for your child's shoes."[2]

Anna was cautious yet curious, but her hope turned quickly to horror when she learned that the shoemaker was a Mormon, and she left the premises immediately. Prejudice against Mormons ran deep in Norway. When the shoes were returned, however, more tracts were tucked inside. Nor was that the last time shoemaker Olaus Johnsen courageously and modestly offered her the truths of the restored gospel of Jesus Christ.

Curiosity eventually drew Anna to attend a meeting in a room on the upper floor of the shoemaker's house. As the daughter of well-respected parents and the widow of a university-trained teacher, she initially resented the primitive environment and the humble nature of the Saints. Joining them, she felt, would be a step downward socially. But after months of inner struggle pondering the new doctrines she was learning and beginning to perceive the rightness in them, Anna said to the Lord, "Must I step down to that? Yes, if it is the truth, I must do so."[3]

Anna was baptized in an icy fjord on April 1, 1881. Throughout her life, she claimed to have felt only warmth on her baptismal day.[4]

But Anna's fears were also borne out. The news of her conversion spread like wildfire from Trondheim to Frøya. Doors were closed to her. Family and friends stopped speaking to her, even her only sister. Her husband's friends turned away from her, and her widow's pension was cut off.

The Trondheim branch became Anna's new family. Shut out from the world that once had welcomed her, Anna turned her devotion and many gifts to blessing the Saints. Her testimony, intelligence, experience, and creative energies helped to invigorate the branch. Before long, she was called to serve in the Relief Society presidency.

Anna's roots in Norway went deep—her forefathers, parents, and husband were buried there, and her loved ones, particularly her sister, Pertroline, still pulled at her heart, even though they rejected her religion. Still, Anna's faith and desire to be with the Saints began to burn in her soul and ultimately won out. Combining her meager savings with contributions from former missionary friends, she bought passage and sailed from Norway with her sons and twenty other Saints in October 1883.

About three weeks later, they arrived safely in Logan, Utah. There she resumed her dressmaking trade. Though the family struggled with poverty, scarcity, severe cold, and injury, she held fast to her faith that the Lord would always provide, and He did, through both the Church organization and the generosity of neighbors. Years later, assistant Church historian Andrew Jenson would say that "Sister Widtsoe [was] one of those strong characters who had set her face like flint to do that which was right."[5]

The blessings of Zion proved to be worth the struggle. Her son John was baptized after requesting the ordinance himself. The completion of the Logan Temple in 1884 was a particularly sweet event. Anna entered the temple to receive the ordinances for herself and have them performed vicariously for her deceased husband. At last the hope of a heavenly reunion was a reality. She cherished the knowledge that her temple covenants would one day reunite her family for eternity. Her joy overflowed when she received news that her sister, Pertroline, had accepted the gospel in Norway and been baptized. Soon her sister joined her in Zion.

Never losing sight of her goal to educate her sons, Anna ensured that they attended school. Eager that they should also acquire cultural polish, she provided them both with lessons in music and painting. She also anticipated helping them pursue higher education. Some who knew of her dreams thought she was unwise to emphasize education above employment for her sons, but her determination enabled the Widtsoe boys to fulfill their father's legacy, even in frontier conditions. In 1891 John graduated from Brigham Young College in Logan and left to further his education at Harvard University. The family worked and sacrificed to pay for his studies. Three years later, John graduated with honors and accepted a teaching position at Utah State Agricultural College (now Utah State University). Osborne graduated as valedictorian of his class at Brigham Young College and planned to attend Harvard in the fall of 1897. A week before he was to leave for the east, however, he accepted a call to preach the gospel in the Sandwich Islands (Hawaii), where he served for more than three years. Mother, aunt, and brother all helped defray Osborne's expenses.

Anna and Pertroline, in their early fifties, returned to their beloved Norway—this time as missionaries, supported financially by John and Osborne. Upon arriving in Copenhagen, Denmark, the sisters sought out the headquarters of the Scandinavian Mission. There they met the mission president, their old friend Anthon L. Skanchy, who years before had baptized Anna. He assigned them to serve in Norway, where prejudice against Mormons had increased in the years of their absence. The testimony of two Norwegian women who had gone to Utah and returned to share their faith made a great impression, doing much to change the prevailing attitude toward the Church. It was said of these sister missionaries: "They awakened interest everywhere. Men might lie, said the people, but these women were likely to tell the truth."[6]

Their efforts and faith yielded unexpected success, and they testified that their prayers were answered many times during the four and a half years they served in Norway. One small miracle came when a boyhood friend of Anna's deceased husband, who was then serving in the Norwegian Parliament, successfully petitioned the government to restore her widow's pension, including payment for the intervening years since she became a Latter-day Saint. At the conclusion of her mission, Anna, "with courage in her heart," explained her son John, "went on August 14, 1907, to the cemetery and stood long by the grave of the schoolmaster, her husband. 'Memories of the past filled my heart and overflowed,' she wrote in her journal."[7]

Anna's life had come full circle. Her final years were warmed by the joy of seeing her sons obtain prestigious academic positions. John served as president of Utah State Agricultural College in

Logan (1907–1916) and the University of Utah (1916–1921). Osborne became president of the Latter-day Saints' University in Salt Lake City. Elder Albert E. Bowen later said, "These two little boys . . . have left a mark among the peoples of this state and of surrounding states and of this country, which anybody would be proud to have made."[8]

Anna passed away before the full impact of her influence could be felt. She died on July 11, 1919, eight years before her son John Andreas Widtsoe was called to be an apostle in the Church she had embraced as a young widow in Norway. Before her passing, Anna testified to her son, "I want to tell you that the most glorious thing that came into my life, was the message delivered to me by the Shoemaker Johnsen of Trondheim. The restored gospel has been the great joy of my life. Please bear that witness for me to all who will listen."[9]

From "If It Is the Truth, I Must Do So," by Kiersten Olson and Clinton D. Christensen, in *Women of Faith in the Latter Days, Volume Three, 1846–1870*, edited by Richard E. Turley Jr. and Brittany A. Chapman (Salt Lake City: Deseret Book, 2014), 263–75.

The Spirit of a Great Teacher

MAUD MAY BABCOCK

Maud May Babcock, a petite woman with a resounding voice, began teaching at the University of Utah in 1892. When she retired forty-six years later, she was known as the "first lady of Utah drama."[1] Her students knew her as an inspired and inspiring teacher who taught them how to connect mind, soul, and body to achieve their full potential.

Former Utah governor Herbert B. Maw often told of how she saved him from his own insecurity when he was about to drop out of the University of Utah. He had to work to support himself, and the only courses compatible with his schedule were in pre-law, but he couldn't imagine himself as a lawyer because he was shy and terrified of speaking in public.

A friend took him to see Maud, who agreed to help him if he promised to try out for her next play. To his astonishment she cast him as the king in *A Midsummer Night's Dream.* When he skipped the first rehearsal, hoping that he might be replaced in the cast,

Maud tracked him down in his morning class and insisted that he give it a try.

Herbert had never taken a course in speech or drama, and his monotone delivery was the first challenge that had to be overcome. He recalled Maud saying, "When you read your lines, pick out the words that put over the idea that you have in mind and *stress* them—make them stand out."[2] For weeks he drove himself and his family crazy as he practiced stressing words.

"But that wasn't the worst of it," he said. "The worst of it was my walking." Maud informed him that to play the part of a king, he had to walk with the dignity of a king. "She held me after every rehearsal," Herbert recalled. "We walked up and down the stage hundreds of times with her by my side and showing me how to put forth my foot and to walk like a king would walk." In frustration he told his teacher that he simply could not act like a king. Her reply was unsympathetic but profound. "I don't want you to act like a king," she said. "You *are* the king, so act like yourself!"[3]

One day they met on campus. Maud said, "I have spent hours . . . teaching you how to walk, and as soon as you get out of my sight, you walk like a nincompoop! I want you to know that every step you take—whether I am around or not—must be the step of a king!"[4]

It was a challenge for Herbert, but after a few weeks a miracle happened. "When I walked on the stage on the opening night of the performance with my queen on my side and lords and beautiful ladies dressed in beautiful gowns following me, I *was* the king! I had learned how to walk with self-control." He concluded, "If I hadn't learned that, I could not possibly have gone on with any success in any line of endeavor that I followed. . . . She talked to me more sternly and harshly than any woman or person has ever talked to me in my life, but I loved it. . . . I sought it because I knew she was wanting to develop me more than anything in the world."[5]

Maud May Babcock believed that students learn best through doing. In an era when it was deemed unfeminine and even dangerous for women to participate in sports and exercise, she donned bloomers and taught physical education and nutrition courses for young women. She also served for many years on the general board of the Young Ladies' Mutual Improvement Association (forerunner to today's Young Women).

In 1909 Maud wrote an article for the *Young Woman's Journal* that expressed her belief that "the great spirit of literature is the spirit of God" and that by teaching with the right spirit a teacher could build testimony even with secular matter. "I feel that the thing to be emphasized here is the importance of the teacher," Maud continued. "Not the importance of the knowledge that she has, but the importance of the Spirit of God that she possesses."[6]

Maud May Babcock demonstrated through her remarkable career an ability to integrate higher education, public service, and religious faith. Her impact can perhaps be best described in the words of Herbert Maw: "To me she was a great woman. No greater person ever lived in my life. No person ever contributed to me what she contributed because she was as she was."[7]

From "'Give Us an Expanding Faith,'" by Laurel Thatcher Ulrich, in *Women of Faith in the Latter Days, Volume Three, 1846–1870*, edited by Richard E. Turley Jr. and Brittany A. Chapman (Salt Lake City: Deseret Book, 2014), 1–12.

The Mother of Canadian Scouting

LOUISA GRANT ALSTON

Louisa Grant Alston and her husband, Joseph, had been married for seventeen years when their lives took an unexpected turn. The couple had built their life together in American Fork, Utah, where Louisa had been raised. Music played an essential role in Louisa's upbringing—she was a talented musician, and her father was a music teacher and the owner of Grant's Music Emporium. Joseph and Louisa were an active part of their community, and they, with their children, had participated in hundreds of musical and social events in the Church and city. Joseph and Louisa had also buried twins in American Fork. In 1899, Louisa was busy raising her eight surviving children when she and her husband received a letter with the well-known Box B return address from President Lorenzo Snow. The letter contained a mission call that would forever change their lives:

"The First Presidency of the Church entered into a contract to build a canal for the Alberta Irrigation Company. . . . In connection with this contract settlements are to be formed to be colonized by our people. Colonization is now going on, as well as work on the canal. But it has been reported to us that some of the immigrants who have gone into that country are not, in every respect, the class of people best adapted to build up a new country, and it therefore becomes necessary, in order that the contract might be satisfactorily filled, to call a certain number of more desirable men to settle on the lands selected by us, and to work on the canal.

"It has been reported to us that your circumstances are such that you can go and settle in this country, and that you are willing to do so. . . . We therefore take pleasure in selecting you and your family to go and help to colonize the place named in the contract."[1]

The place was Magrath, located in the Northwest Territories of Canada. Louisa, along with their seven daughters and one son, joined Joseph at their new home in June 1890. Louisa described the country as "beautiful, [with] tall grass everywhere" but was less impressed with their living accommodations. Joseph, "always a bit of a practical joker," had written to the family "that he had purchased a building known as the King's Hotel for a dwelling." Thinking of hotels as they knew them, Louisa and the children supposed it would have a number of rooms. Louisa wrote that they "were a bit surprised, disappointed and somewhat disgusted to find a one-room shack with a tent pitched beside it."[2]

Joseph had purchased the building for forty dollars from the North West Mounted Police, who had used it as a "barrick's barn," and "had it moved onto a ten-acre block he had purchased."[3] Louisa noted that the property had "no fence, not even a post for miles around, but true enough inscribed across the front was King's

Hotel, put there by boys who bunked in it, while working on construction of [the] canal."[4]

Settling in, Louisa became a driving force for music in the community of Magrath. She recalled that "it wasn't long until I began a very busy life, first organist of the ward and as there weren't many musicians, was called to help all of the organizations, took many important parts and have been a very busy woman."[5] She brought the first organ to town and for years played for church meetings and community events. She also started the first marching band, a fife and drum combination, and served as the stake Primary music leader from 1904 to 1930. But music would not be Louisa's only legacy.

Louisa had been active in the Primary organization from its earliest days, serving in her ward Primary presidency in both American Fork and McGrath. From her love of teaching Christian principles to youth, teaching them to love music, and testifying to them of the restored gospel of Jesus Christ also came "an active interest in the boys through her work in the Primary association."[6] In 1913, the Church officially adopted the Boy Scout program to help train young men to be responsible reliable, upstanding citizens. So

when Scouting came to Magrath the following spring, Louisa, in true pioneering spirit, agreed to serve as the Assistant Scoutmaster for approximately twenty-five boys. A few months later, Great Britain declared war on Germany, and as citizens of the British Empire, tens of thousands of Canadian men joined the army. At the age of fifty-two, Louisa became Canada's first female Scoutmaster.

Under Louisa's leadership, the troop had annual outings and campouts, learned about nature and wildlife, and focused on obeying the Scout law. But the troop's principal work was in their association with the Red Cross in supporting the war effort during World War I. When the Duke of Devonshire, Sir Victor Christian William Cavendish, toured the western provinces of Canada in 1917, Louisa was chosen to lead the Scouts from Magrath and the surrounding towns to meet him. A newspaper reported: "It was a stormy day . . . and most of the Scouts from adjacent towns backed out, but not Magrath; [Louisa] would have none of that; every boy who was able to go must go. She and her Scouts boarded the train and picked up a few more as the train proceeded to Lethbridge, until there were 60 of them. The Governor-General had heard of her work and he gave the boys a special audience, shook hands with them and had his picture taken with them. He said of the boys: 'Well, that's as fine a group of lads as I ever saw. What a blessing it is to you boys to have a woman to give you this training when the boys who should be training you are away at war. Remember, that obedience is the keynote of success.'"[7]

A month later, the duke appointed Louisa a Scout Commissioner, the first time such a distinction was conferred on a woman. Her duties took her to various towns in southern Alberta and to international jamborees, where she taught the values of Scouting and influenced hundreds of young men. Louisa also had the honor of having twelve of her Scouts chosen to act as a guard of honor to the Prince of Wales, who later became King Edward VIII, on his visit to Lethbridge. After Louisa's husband of forty-two years passed away, she wrote in her journal, "I ought to record here that I am a widow, my husband died on the 31st of December, 1924, of heart failure. . . . This is one reason that this record is so incomplete. It seems that my life was useless and that the end was so near that there was nothing to write."[8]

But Louisa was far from useless. In 1939 she was awarded the Boy Scouts of Canada Medal of Merit for her "particularly fine service" as "one of the pioneers of Scouting in Canada."[9] She continued to teach music lessons, promote stage plays, and participate in community events and Scouting into her eighties. Louisa passed away at the age of eighty-four, on October 26, 1945, in Magrath, the adopted town she had served so well. Perhaps the greatest tribute she would receive came sixty-six years later, in 2011, when Louisa Grant Alston was posthumously honored as the mother of Canadian Scouting and the Legislative Assembly of Alberta named a community Scout park in Magrath after her.

From "Mother of Canadian Scouting," by William Ray Alston, in *Women of Faith in the Latter Days, Volume Three, 1846–1870*, edited by Richard E. Turley Jr. and Brittany A. Chapman (Salt Lake City: Deseret Book, 2014), eBook.

STEADFAST IN ALL THINGS

Trust in the Lord

BELINDA MARDEN PRATT

Belinda Marden Pratt wrote a sketch of her life in a letter written two days before her death on July 24, 1882. Ending mid-sentence, she urged her eldest son, "Nephi will you, if you can, fill it in from here?"[1] Her writing evidenced her dedication, faith during trials, and firm defense of the religious principles she held dear to her heart.

Belinda, the fourteenth child of John and Rachel Marden, was born on Christmas Eve 1820. She described her parents as "strictly moral and members of the Congregational Church." At the age of nineteen, Belinda married Benjamin Hilton, but there were significant differences between the two. Recalling that time in her life, Belinda said, "My husband was an infidel and unbelieving in most things pertaining to religion, while I was continually ambitious to find the right kind of religion, never feeling assured that those I was acquainted with were right."[2]

Unsettled by her feelings, Belinda quietly continued her search for the truth, and in 1843 her attention was drawn to a handbill advertising a Latter-day Saint preacher. Belinda and her husband arrived and found the elder in prayer. "And such a prayer!" she recalled. "We stood in the aisle till he finished. I think the light of heaven rested down upon me for the joy and peace I experienced was inexpressible. We attended the three meetings, morning, afternoon, and evening. I had an overwhelming testimony that what he preached was true and was so rejoiced that I seemed to myself light as air, as though my feet scarcely touched the ground."[3]

Her joy was tempered by her husband's lack of enthusiasm. "I prayed often and much and felt great concern because my husband took so different a view of it from what I did. I wrote to my sisters, they thought I must be crazy. All opposed me and all I could do was to continually cry to the Lord. We continued to attend the meetings and one day in March my husband came home at an unusual hour and told me he was so wrought upon that he could not work or sleep and he would have to go and get baptized. Didn't my heart rejoice? Then I could go and O what joy!"[4]

Both Belinda and Benjamin were baptized in Boston Harbor, in water "so cold the ice had to be broken and held back with poles while we went in," Belinda recalled. Unfortunately Benjamin's faith soon began to waver, and he became increasingly bitter against the Church. Belinda remained faithful and firm in her testimony and began to fear her husband's anger and persecution at her continued association with the Saints.

"He let me have no peace day and night, forbid me going to meeting or having any association with the Mormons as he chose to call them. I did not know what I was going to do or how I could live under the pressure, for all my relatives were as bitter as he was. All I could do was to pray continually to the Lord and he surely heard my prayers."[5]

Lyman Wight, who was preaching in the area, heard of Belinda's struggles and counseled her to join the Saints in Nauvoo. When Belinda told him that she did not have the funds to travel that distance, Elder Wight promised her that if she were to go, she would "never see the day [she] would be sorry for it."[6] He suggested that she seek help from a sister in Utica, New York, who could provide assistance with traveling expenses.

Belinda left Boston in July of 1844 under the guise of visiting relatives. "When the morning came for me to start on my visit, Mr. Hilton went with me to the depot and waited till the train started. Of course I had to start north instead of west," Belinda recounted.

"When I found myself alone at the first station I ordered my trunk and told the conductor I would have to go back to Boston."

From there, Belinda immediately started for Utica, as Elder Wight had directed. "My heart was filled with joy and thanksgiving, for I never doubted for one moment but what I should get along all right and that God would bless me. All the sorrow I had was for [Mr. Hilton] and I pitied him more than I can express on paper."[7] Traveling under a false name to prevent her husband and family from following her, Belinda journeyed the fifteen hundred miles to Nauvoo.

Upon reaching Nauvoo, Belinda worked as a dressmaker to support herself. She accepted the teachings of the Prophet Joseph Smith but struggled with the practice of polygamy: "A good sister where I was stopping called in Pres. Young to talk to me. He instructed me in the principle, and desiring with all my heart to understand the truth, I testify that the Holy Spirit of God rested down upon me and it was made plain to my understanding that it was a divine principle, and with great joy of heart I accepted it. And never from that time to this, 1884, has there been a doubt in my mind concerning it."[8]

Belinda's husband obtained a divorce, and she was subsequently sealed to Parley P. Pratt as his sixth wife in 1844.

Belinda found strength while crossing the plains through her association with Parley's other wives. Ann Agatha Walker, Parley's tenth wife, eulogized Belinda: "A better, or more noble woman I never knew. In our traveling together we sometimes took turns— she driving one day and I the next. She had a delicate babe and when she drove I took care of it, and through all the vicissitudes of our life together we have loved and respected each other greatly, and she has always been very near and dear to me and her children are next to my own."[9]

Despite the trials of pioneer life, Belinda was content. She wrote to her sister in 1854: "I have a good and virtuous husband whom I love. We have four little children which are mutually and inexpressibly dear to us."[10]

The death of her beloved husband three years later was excruciating for Belinda. Daughter Isabella wrote: "Belinda passed through the unspeakable grief of losing her husband by assassination while he was on a mission in 1857. Left with a family of little children unprovided [for] and unprotected, she struggled through years of more than ordinary hardships and privations. She was an educated, refined and gentle woman, full of sympathy, generosity and kindness. She taught school, made dresses, took boarders. The struggle was a brave one."[11]

From "The Joy and Peace I Experienced Was Inexpressible," by Taunalyn Ford Rutherford, in *Women of Faith in the Latter Days, Volume One, 1775–1820*, edited by Richard E. Turley Jr. and Brittany A. Chapman (Salt Lake City: Deseret Book, 2011), 233–45.

A Mother in Zion

ELIZABETH HARRISON GODDARD

Elizabeth Harrison was born in Leicester, England, in 1817, the second of three children born to John and Elizabeth Pipes Harrison. Her parents were not particularly religious but taught their daughter principles of honesty, truthfulness, and virtue. And they taught her to pray. Of her childhood Elizabeth wrote, "These good principles being early instilled in my mind, I became naturally inclined to be religious, keeping the Sabbath Day holy, and attending a place of worship."[1]

Elizabeth married George Goddard at age twenty-two and stopped attending the Methodist church in order to attend the local Baptist church, where her husband was a deacon. Although they faithfully attended church services together, Elizabeth reflected, "I agreed to go with him rather than be separated, but I must say I did not enjoy myself as well."[2]

Eventually, both Elizabeth and George began to feel that something was lacking, particularly with regard to the doctrine of baptism. Elizabeth had a desire to be baptized by immersion as the

Savior had. So when the family came in contact with missionaries from The Church of Jesus Christ of Latter-day Saints, they recognized the teachings of the Savior. George recounted in his journal, "I had entertained a very poor opinion of the Mormon people as a religious body. The first discourse I ever heard fully convinced me . . . and I promised to go again."[3]

Elizabeth was concerned about her husband getting involved with the Mormons. When she inquired about his reaction to their discourse, "He replied that if he had never heard the Gospel before, he had heard it that night, and said he intended going again."[4] The missionaries left with her a copy of the Book of Mormon and *The Voice of Warning*, by Elder Parley P. Pratt, which Elizabeth found convincing. She and her husband were baptized the following evening.

George was asked by the elders to preach the restored gospel in the marketplace every week. Consequently his customers ceased to patronize his store, and his business was in danger of failing. The reaction from George and Elizabeth's parents and siblings was similarly adverse. Elizabeth recalled, "When it was known we had embraced Mormonism there was a great disgust about it by our relatives and friends, so much so that one of my husband's brothers said he would rather pay our passage to America where Mormons flourished like buttercups and where fools and bigots dwelled in undisturbed serenity"—presumably to avoid the possibility of being connected in any way to the couple's newly embraced religion.[5] True to his word, George's brother paid fifty pounds to settle George's debts in England and pay for the family's passage to America.

In early October 1851 George and Elizabeth boarded the *Essex,*
bound for America. They had with them seven of their eight children—their fifth child, Annie, having died at three days of age—
and Elizabeth was pregnant again. Although she described the
voyage as favorable, after they had been "three weeks on the ocean
a son was born but only lived ½ an hour, being somewhat prema-
ture." "Fortunately," Elizabeth wrote, "the sea was calm and warm
as we were passing by the West India Islands, but my dear babe had
to be consigned to a watery grave. The captain was very kind lend-
ing me things to add to my comfort, and sent the ship's carpenter
to put in a glass door in a port hole near to my bed so that I could
have a little breeze from the sea. I had neither doctor nor nurse, but
my husband. But I got along splendidly."[6]

After nine weeks on the *Essex,* the family arrived in New
Orleans and then, advised not to stay there with young children,
they traveled by steamer up the Mississippi. Outside of Memphis,
their steamer hit a snag that took out one of the paddle wheels, and
the boat had to be towed in. During the week while the steamer

was being repaired, nineteen-month-old Cornelius, the youngest of the surviving children, died. Elizabeth felt that his health had been weakened by the change of climate and by cutting a number of teeth while they were at sea. She also believed that Memphis was "an unhealthy place" and that these conditions had contributed to his death. Elizabeth's heartbreak was multiplied when they took the child's body to be buried and discovered that the grave had not yet been dug. With great sorrow Elizabeth was forced to "leave him in the dead house [where] they assured me that the interment would be attended to. It was hard but had to submit as the boat was ready to start again."[7]

The family arrived in St. Louis on New Year's Day. Elizabeth's faith and optimistic spirit shone through despite her recent hardship. She wrote: "We found a good sized room with a fireplace in it, which was in the cold month of January. My dear little Betsy took sick and died. She was about 4 years old. She wanted to live and said, 'Mama, make me well. I want to go to the Valley,' but she went into convulsions and died. Thus I had to lay another of my dear ones away. My husband would not allow me to go and see her consigned to Mother Earth, for I was not well and the weather very cold."[8]

George and Elizabeth forged ahead. The family stayed in St. Louis until May, and George, who peddled items to pay the rent, was blessed to trade for a stock of "a great many thousand" needles.[9] Then they took a steamer to Council Bluffs, Iowa. With many people there bound for California and Salt Lake City, it was a busy place to buy, sell, and trade. George Goddard wrote: "To make the most of the situation with a view of securing our own outfit, we rigged up two of our children with a supply of needles and a few other articles, with instructions to call at every house, and sell needles at the rate of three papers for twenty-five cents. While they were going through one street, I visited another, and at the close of each day, we deposited the amount of our sales with my wife. Nearly every family in Bluff City bought needles of us, which formed the chief basis of our capital for the purchase of our oxen, wagon, etc. . . . We had every reason to believe that the means deposited with my wife daily, was added to or multiplied while in her possession, for on several occasions we found a larger sum than was previously deposited, which verified the truth of the adage: 'The Lord helps those who help themselves.'"[10]

They soon procured the needed supplies and joined the John Tidwell Company to cross the plains. The company experienced the usual challenges of plains travel: breakdown of equipment and wagons, sick animals, locating suitable campsites, keeping members cooperating, covering adequate distances each day, and finding food. There were leadership meetings, religious services, and baptisms. A few weeks into the trek, cholera struck the camp. In a matter of days, three of Elizabeth's five remaining children became gravely ill. Elizabeth remembered: "Daughter Eliza was seized with it. Afterwards our eldest son, George, was attacked, and then our little Henry, about 3 years old, who did not live many hours. The others lingered, George seemed to improve and would be dressed to go and see some children baptized, but I think he took cold and had a relapse and we had to part with him. Dear Eliza was the only one who recovered but was very weak for some time." The epidemic lasted a month and devastated the company, taking lives both young and old. Elizabeth commented, "Some mothers and fathers were taken away with this scourge. I felt I would rather part with my children, than be taken away from them."[11]

The family finally arrived in the Salt Lake Valley in September of 1852, nearly a year after their departure from England. Elizabeth had lost five of her children in their journey to join with the Saints.

The family lived in a borrowed tent until they could purchase a home in exchange for their two yoke of oxen and a cow. Two more cows were given to Brother Green, their teamster. George took their last cow to the Tithing Office. With winter coming Elizabeth traded the dog she had brought from Kanesville for ten bushels of potatoes and flavored them with mushrooms found on their property. Elizabeth was undaunted. "We soon got comforts around us," she wrote, "my husband being energetic and willing to do anything that presented to him to get a living so that we were blest with the comforts of life."[12]

George's needles, though a little rusty, were items much needed by most families in the Salt Lake Valley. He sold notions from a street stall until Thomas McKenzie vacated his store to move to the country.[13] Four more children were added to their family, although heartache once more lay around the corner when John Goddard, then sixteen, drowned in the Jordan River. Soon thereafter six-month-old son Alma passed away. Of Elizabeth and George's thirteen children, only five survived to adulthood.

Elizabeth was deeply involved in Relief Society and in the lives of many people in Salt Lake City, going to surprise birthday parties, attending concerts at the Assembly Hall, and visiting family members. She loved her husband dearly and supported him in his many callings. He passed away in 1899, and many friends and family comforted Elizabeth at his funeral. On April 12, 1903, Elizabeth, aged eighty-six, followed her husband to "the realms above."[14] In an obituary of Elizabeth Goddard, the *Woman's Exponent* praised her: "She was faithful, true, patient and self-sacrificing, devoted to her husband and children, yet fulfilling many other duties. She was a Saint in the strict sense of the word."[15]

From "A Legacy of Hope, and Faith, and Love," by Madelyn Silver Palmer, in *Women of Faith in the Latter Days, Volume One, 1775–1820,* edited by Richard E. Turley Jr. and Brittany A. Chapman (Salt Lake City: Deseret Book, 2011), 41–53.

A Paisley Shawl

RACHEL EMMA WOOLLEY SIMMONS

Rachel Emma Woolley was not yet two years old when her Quaker parents, Edwin Dilworth and Mary Wickersham Woolley, chose to become members of The Church of Jesus Christ of Latter-day Saints. In 1839, the family gathered to Nauvoo, where they all came down with a sickness called ague—probably malaria—that was prevalent in the city at the time. Although she was quite young, Rachel recalled lying "in a trundle bed with my brothers, and all shaking until it seemed as if our teeth would come out. The chill would last for hours, then the fever was just as hard as the chill."[1]

Joseph and Hyrum Smith were frequent visitors at the Woolley home in Nauvoo, and the family enjoyed a close association with the Prophet. His martyrdom left an indelible impression on the young girl. A few months later she celebrated her eighth birthday and was baptized in the Mississippi River.

After the exodus from Nauvoo, the family remained in Winter Quarters until May 1849. Rachel's later writings reveal the adventures of life on the trail for a young pioneer girl. The family began their journey across the plains to the Salt Lake Valley with three wagons and a horse-drawn buggy for her mother, who was in delicate health. Rachel, who turned twelve on the trek, was given the responsibility of driving the buggy. "I did so in fear and trembling, as one of the horses was very vicious," she recalled.[2] Another chore assigned to Rachel was to collect buffalo chips to burn in the campfires. Once, the buffalo chips "were very thick in a certain place close to the road," she wrote. "I thought I was in luck, but I soon found out the cause. I was picking up as fast as I could when all at once I heard the rattle of a snake. I looked to see in what direction it was and there he was in a hole almost at my feet. I did not stop for any more chips at that time. That was the second escape I had of being bitten by a rattle snake. . . . I acknowledge the hand of the Lord in it."[3]

Some incidents, such as driving over Rocky Ridge, planted themselves in her memory. The family had an old pig that was ready to give birth and rode in the buggy Rachel was driving. "Father was very anxious to save the little pigs, but they all died in consequence of the rough road," she recalled. "I was so glad when we camped that night. I was so completely tired out, with the road and the frisky horse."[4]

Certainly the determination and courage gained from her pioneer experiences proved invaluable later in life. In 1850, a few years after her arrival in the Salt Lake Valley, Rachel met Joseph Marcellus Simmons, a California-bound gold miner who had stopped in Utah to replenish his supplies. While passing through Salt Lake City, he became interested in the Church and remained as a boarder in the Woolley home. Rachel remembered, "He told me afterwards that he had a motive in staying. He said he loved me the first time he seen me and came with the determination to make me his wife."[5] Joseph and Rachel were married by Brigham Young a year later, in 1851.

Over the next twenty-one years, Joseph and Rachel were blessed with ten children. Not long after she joined other women of Utah in casting votes for the first time, Rachel became a widow. She recounted that she had gone to city hall to vote and returned home five minutes later to find that her husband had experienced "a very bad spell. I think he was struck with death then, but he didn't die until [two days later]." She was just thirty-five years old with ten children to support, ages six months to nineteen years. The family's financial situation at that time was such that Rachel wrote, "[We] were out of everything. Father had to get us things to go to the funeral."[6]

Once again the hand of the Lord directed Rachel's path. At the request of Zina D. H. Young, one of Utah's leading women, Rachel agreed to take medical training as a midwife but not without hesitation. Rachel wrote, "I told Sister Zina I couldn't do so for I hadn't the means," but Zina assured her that members of the Relief Society would fund her schooling to provide her with a profession so she could support herself.[7] In 1883 Rachel noted: "I paid to the Relief Society twenty-one dollars and a half today, being money I borrowed to attend a course of lectures on midwifery. . . . I looked upon it as a loan and as such paid it."[8]

"Aunt Rachel," as she was lovingly called by her patients, was dedicated to her calling. One Christmas her children gave her a

beautiful woolen paisley shawl, which she often used to wrap new-borns. She penned a tribute to this shawl, calling it her "old and honored friend." She wrote, "You have ministered to the aged and given warmth to the newly born. You have been at my side through many a hard fought battle, always ready to serve."[9]

For nearly forty years, the woman who began her career as a destitute young widow with a large family to support continued her service as a midwife, safely delivering hundreds of babies. On one occasion she wrote in her journal: "I have been the instrument in the Lord's hand of bringing two children into the world today. . . . I hope the Lord will bless me in the future as he has in the past, for I realize that without his help I can do nothing. His is the honor and the glory for all the work of my hands."[10]

Among those Rachel helped to welcome into the world were most of her own grandchildren, great-grandchildren, and a nephew, Spencer Woolley Kimball, who became the twelfth president of the Church. A grandson paid this tribute: "She did not seem to be subject to the distractions and vicissitudes of life, but was always calm, kind, loving and sympathetic." She lived a life of "courage, dignity and honor."[11]

From "'The Lord Helps Us in Small Things As Well As Large,'" by Laura F. Willes, in *Women of Faith in the Latter Days, Volume Two, 1821–1845*, edited by Richard E. Turley Jr. and Brittany A. Chapman (Salt Lake City: Deseret Book, 2012), 333–49.

Footprints of Faith

JANETTA ANN McBRIDE FERRIN

Janetta Ann McBride was born in Churchtown, Lancashire, England, on Christmas Eve 1839, when The Church of Jesus Christ of Latter-day Saints was just beginning its rapid expansion in the British Isles. Her parents were among the first converts to the Church in Britain, and Janetta's youth was marked by close associations with early Church leaders. "The elders used to stay with my parents and missionary meetings were held in our home," she recalled. "My mother would make the bread for the sacrament for the meetings."[1]

About the time of Janetta's first birthday, her father received a letter from family friend Heber C. Kimball urging the McBrides to gather with the Saints when their circumstances permitted. More than a decade and a half passed before gathering became a reality for the family. Janetta described how eager the members of the family were to make the journey, not fully realizing the great sacrifice that would be required. "We had always looked forward to the time when we could go to Utah," she wrote. "In the spring of 1856 we received word that we could go by the [Perpetual] Emigration Fund, if we would go with the handcart company. . . . By going this way we could travel from Liverpool to Salt Lake City, Utah, for forty-five dollars. This was a big savings, but for the seven of us, my parents and five children, it was still quite a bit."[2]

Janetta was sixteen years old when she and her family made the long-anticipated journey to America. Almost immediately there were signs of impending trouble. "When we arrived in Iowa, every-thing was to be ready for us to travel on," she recalled, "but through some mistake nothing was ready. We walked in heavy rain and waded creeks in mud. Three weeks later the handcarts were ready."[3]

The delay would soon prove fatal for some of those Saints who, undaunted by the inadequate preparations, steadfastly built handcarts themselves. Assigned to the ill-fated Martin Handcart Company, Janetta recorded that some of "the missionaries tried to talk us into staying until spring, since it was a month later than we should have started, but we voted to go on."[4]

The company's vote to continue to Utah despite the late start and its decision to discard extra supplies, particularly clothes and bedding, to lighten the load showed the Saints' confidence and opti-mism at the outset, but their hardships quickly became more severe. Janetta's mother became sick, and her father's health also quickly failed. Janetta and her younger brother Heber pulled their handcart containing the family's supplies while their parents alternated riding on the cart with their younger sister Maggie. As conditions wors-ened, the pioneers began to die of hunger, fatigue, and exposure. Heber struggled to depict the burden he and Janetta shouldered, saying, "No tongue nor pen could tell what my sister [Janetta] and I passed through. . . . It seemed as though death would be a blessing, for we used to pray that we might die to get out of our misery, for by this time it was getting very cold weather and our clothing almost worn out and not enough of bedclothes to keep us warm."[5]

Despite her trials, Janetta pressed on with faith and perseverance beyond her years. Her role in her family's survival became nothing short of heroic when they reached the banks of the North Platte River on October 19, 1856. Janetta recalled: "It was freezing and the river was very wide. I crossed it with my handcart and had to go back and haul my mother across and get the children across, and it was getting dark and very cold and my clothes were wet."[6]

Young Janetta dodged dangerous chunks of ice and braved the chest-deep river to pull her family across, and her starving father rallied strength beyond his own and "worked all day pulling, pushing, wading through the icy river," making "about twenty-five trips across the river helping to get all the people and carts across."[7] In an effort that cost him his life, her father "never stopped until the last person and all carts were across."[8]

Janetta pushed her handcart the remaining mile to camp, her wet dress freezing on her body in the biting winds of the early winter snowstorm. Despite her exhaustion, she gathered wood for the fire and cooked the half pound of flour the family had been allotted for the day. Heber recalled, "With cold wind blowing and snow drifting, my sister [Janetta] and I let our parents have our blanket and we would lie down without any covering."[9]

Janetta always remembered her father's abiding faith even in his final hours that night as he sang the hymn "O Zion." She said, "I think he sang the song through, and then we led him to the wagon. That was the last I saw of him alive. He died in the wagon the next day and they buried him that night with 14 others, all in the same grave."[10] Young Janetta took the lead in caring for her family. She struggled to pull her handcart through the deepening snow and desperately coaxed her starving younger siblings onward with biscuit crumbs saved from her own meager rations. Her brother Peter recalled that Janetta "had all the worries of taking care of us children. She carried water from the river for cooking purposes, her shoes gave out and she walked through the snow barefoot, actually leaving bloody tracks in the snow."[11] Even after the rescue wagons arrived, Janetta walked the rest of the way "up the steep mountain, barefoot with snow two or three feet deep."[12]

Janetta's surviving family members rejoiced in their long-awaited arrival in Salt Lake City on November 30, 1856. They were immediately sent to Ogden, where widower Samuel Ferrin kindly provided for them in exchange for help with cooking and cleaning. The dirt roof in their small one-room home leaked mud, and the family continued to suffer sickness, hunger, and privation throughout the winter. Janetta's brother Ether asked, "Is this Zion to live in such a place as this?" Despite all the trials they had passed through, however, their mother faithfully responded, "Never mind, the Lord will provide."[13]

Springtime brought new beginnings. Romance quickly blossomed between Janetta and Samuel's son Jacob. They were married on March 29, 1857, and Janetta's widowed mother married Samuel shortly thereafter.

Janetta and Jacob's married life was marked by great industry, harmony, and the birth of eleven children in twenty-four years. In

1881, Janetta once again answered the call of a prophet, President John Taylor, to be a pioneer in helping settle the Gila Valley in Arizona. This time Janetta ensured that they were well prepared for the thousand-mile journey, driving a team all the way with a baby in her arms. Although her husband's health was not good, the family enjoyed a short time of peace in their new home in Pima, but it was not to last. Janetta wrote, "We liked Pima and the nice warm climate. Jacob's health was better and it seemed that we were going to be happy here, but our happiness was short-lived: 6 months after we had settled there, my husband was killed by the Apache Indians."[14]

She wrote nothing else of the tragic loss that left her a widow at the age of forty-three with eight children still in her care. The men of the town helped her sons build a one-room adobe house in which they lived for many years, and she relied on her skills as a seamstress to help earn a living. She never complained nor wavered in her devotion to the gospel, raising all of her children to be faithful Latter-day Saints and leaving a lasting legacy of steadfast faith. At the time of her death, at the age of eighty-five, the woman who had risked her life as a teenage girl crossing the plains had eighty-five grandchildren, 150 great-grandchildren, and nine great-great-grandchildren. Many thousands of her descendants today enjoy the blessings of the gospel because of her courage.

From "All Kinds of Trials and Hardships," by Rebekah Ryan Clark and Marcus Patrick Ryan, in *Women of Faith in the Latter Days, Volume Two, 1821–1845*, edited by Richard E. Turley Jr. and Brittany A. Chapman (Salt Lake City: Deseret Book, 2012), 61–75.

Notes

CHAPTER 1 • SUSANAH STONE LLOYD

1. Susanah Stone Lloyd, "The Sketch of Susanna Stone Lloyd," in Information on Thomas and Susanna Lloyd, ca. 1915, Typescript, p. 2, Church History Library, The Church of Jesus Christ of Latter-day Saints, Salt Lake City, Utah.
2. Lloyd, "Sketch," 2.
3. Lloyd, "Sketch," 2.
4. Lloyd, "Sketch," 2.
5. Lloyd, "Sketch," 2.
6. Mary Ellen W. Smoot, "Developing Inner Strength," *Ensign*, May 2002, 13.

CHAPTER 2 • LAURA CLARK PHELPS

1. Morris Calvin Phelps, "Life History of Laura Clark," Typescript, p. 1, Church History Library, The Church of Jesus Christ of Latter-day Saints, Salt Lake City, Utah.
2. Mary Ann Phelps Rich, "Early History," in *Autobiography of Mary Ann Phelps Rich*, Microfilm of typescript, p. 6, Family History Library, The Church of Jesus Christ of Latter-day Saints, Salt Lake City, Utah.
3. Rich, "Early History," 6.
4. Heber C. Kimball, *President Heber C. Kimball's Journal* (Salt Lake City, UT: Juvenile Instructor Office, 1882; Heber City, UT: Archive Publishers, 2003), 87.
5. Heber C. Kimball, "Obituary," *Times and Seasons* 3, no. 9 (March 1, 1842): 714.
6. Parley P. Pratt, *Autobiography of Parley Parker Pratt*, ed. Parley P. Pratt Jr. (Chicago: Law, King, and Law, 1888), 266–67.
7. Pratt, *Autobiography*, 274.
8. Mary Ann Phelps Rich, "A Hazardous Mission of Love," in *Autobiography of Mary Ann Phelps Rich*, Microfilm of typescript, pp. 9–10, Family History Library.
9. Pratt, *Autobiography*, 287.
10. Rich, "Hazardous Mission," 10.
11. Rich, "Hazardous Mission," 11.
12. Rich, "Hazardous Mission," 12.

13. Mary Ann Phelps Rich, "A Happy Reunion," in *Autobiography of Mary Ann Phelps Rich*, Microfilm of typescript, p. 14, Family History Library; spelling modernized.
14. Kimball, "Obituary," 713.
15. Joseph Smith, quoted in Rich, "Happy Reunion," 14.
16. *History of The Church of Jesus Christ of Latter-day Saints*, ed. B. H. Roberts, 2nd ed. rev., 7 vols. (Salt Lake City, UT: The Church of Jesus Christ of Latter-day Saints, 1932–51), 4:513.

CHAPTER 3 • ROSA CLARA FRIEDLANDER LOGIE

1. Laura Clara Logie Timpson, "A Brief History of the Lives of Charles Joseph Gordon Logie & Rosa Clara Friedlander Logie," 1965, Photocopy of typescript, private possession. The date of the baptism is not recorded, but the missionaries who taught and baptized Charles Logie did not arrive in Australia until the end of March 1853.
2. Augustus A. Farnham, Journals, 1852–1856, May 21, 1853, vol. 1, Holograph, Church History Library, The Church of Jesus Christ of Latter-day Saints, Salt Lake City, Utah; spelling, punctuation, capitalization, and grammar modernized.
3. The atoll is known today as Manuae Atoll.
4. Benjamin Franklin Pond, Autobiography, 1895, Microform, Library of Congress. Typescript of applicable portion available as "Wreck of the *Julia Ann*," Mormon Migration Database, Brigham Young University, Provo, Utah, accessed September 1, 2015, http://mormonmigration.lib.byu.edu.
5. John McCarthy to [George Q.] Cannon, April 25, 1856, in "Editor of the Standard," *Deseret News [Weekly]*, July 2, 1856.
6. Timpson, "Brief History," 2.
7. Peter Penfold to Charles Penfold, February 17, 1856, in *Zion's Watchman* 2, no. 5 (May 24, 1856): 78.
8. Penfold to Penfold, February 17, 1856, 17.
9. John Penfold to Augustus Farnham, March 21, 1856, in *Zion's Watchman* 2, no. 5 (May 24, 1856): 70.

CHAPTER 4 • MARY ROSELIA COOK MCCANN

1. Mrs. Hyrum J. McCann, "A Sketch of My Life for Jean," Holograph, pp. 3–4, Utah State Historical Society, Salt Lake City, Utah; spelling, punctuation, and grammar modernized in quotations from this document.
2. McCann, "Sketch of My Life," 7.
3. McCann, "Sketch of My Life," 16.
4. McCann, "Sketch of My Life," 16.
5. McCann, "Sketch of My Life," 34.
6. McCann, "Sketch of My Life," 35.
7. McCann, "Sketch of My Life," 41.
8. McCann, "Sketch of My Life," 42.
9. McCann, "Sketch of My Life," 42.
10. McCann, "Sketch of My Life," 67–68.

CHAPTER 5 • MARY GOBLE PAY

1. Mary Goble Pay, Autobiography, 1903, Holograph, p. 102, private possession; spelling, capitalization, and punctuation modernized in quotations from this document.

2. Pay, *Autobiography*, 103. The "Hunt Wagon Company Journal" records for October 28: "Brothers Joseph W. Young and two other brethren arrived in camp in the evening from the Valley. This caused a general rejoicing throughout the camp, though the tidings of the snow extending westward for forty or fifty miles, was not encouraging. The handcart companies had been supplied with food and clothing and the condition of the wagon companies would be reported to the Valley speedily, as the brethren traveling with teams were also getting short of provisions." Journal History of The Church of Jesus Christ of Latter-day Saints, p. 33, Church History Library, The Church of Jesus Christ of Latter-day Saints, Salt Lake City, Utah.

3. Pay, *Autobiography*, 101. The company journal records that "the infant child of William Goble" died at Greasewood Creek on November 3 at 9 o'clock P.M. "Hunt Wagon Company Journal," November 3, 1856, p. 34.

4. Pay, *Autobiography*, 105.

5. Four-year-old James died November 6 while the company was at Devil's Gate. "Hunt Wagon Company Journal," 35; Pay, *Autobiography*, 102.

6. Pay, *Autobiography*, 103.

7. Mary Goble Pay, "Life of Mary Goble Pay," Typescript, p. 3, private possession.

8. Pay, *Autobiography*, 103.

9. Pay, *Autobiography*, 109. A spider was a cast-iron frying pan, originally made with feet to stand among coals.

10. Mary Goble Pay, interview by Philip LeRoy Pay, transcribed by Leon R. Pay, pp. 1–2, Family records, in private possession.

11. Mary received this patriarchal blessing from Jacob G. Bigler in February 1895 in Nephi, Utah. It is on file at the Church History Library; spelling modernized.

12. Phillip LeRoy Pay, "Dreams of Mary Goble Pay," Typescript, p. 1, photocopy in private possession.

13. Phillip LeRoy Pay, interview by Leon R. Pay, Holograph, pp. 3–4, Family records, photocopy in private possession; spelling, capitalization, and punctuation modernized.

CHAPTER 6 · DIANTHA MORLEY BILLINGS

1. At that time called the Church of Christ.

2. Elizabeth Ann Whitney, "Leaf from an Autobiography," *Woman's Exponent* 7 (November 15, 1878): 91.

3. Eunice Billings Warner Snow, "Eunice Billings Warner Snow Tells Her Own Story," ca. 1910–1914, ed. Marba Peck Hale, Typescript, p. 1, L. Tom Perry Special Collections, Harold B. Lee Library, Brigham Young University, Provo, Utah.

4. Snow, "Eunice Billings Warner Snow," 1.

5. Lucinda Snow, "Eliza Ann Carter Snow: A Biographical Sketch," *Woman's Exponent* 25 (April 15, 1897): 134–35. The mob entered Far West on November 1, 1838.

6. Helen Mar Whitney, "Scenes and Incidents at Winter Quarters," *Woman's Exponent* 13 (December 1, 1884): 98.

7. Eunice Billings Snow, "Sketches from the Life of Eunice Billings Snow," *Woman's Exponent* 40 (January 1, 1912): 47.

8. Thomas Bullock, June 1, 1848, Journals 1843–1849, Church History Library, The Church of Jesus Christ of Latter-day Saints, Salt Lake City, Utah.

9. Eunice Billings Snow, "A Sketch of the Life of Eunice Billings Snow," *Woman's Exponent* 39 (September 1, 1910): 23.

10. Emmeline B. Wells, "History of the Relief Society," *Woman's Exponent* 32 (June 1, 1903): 6.

Chapter 7 · Elizabeth Ann Claridge McCune

1. "From an Adobe Hut to a Mansion of Brick and Stone," *Deseret Evening News,* June 6, 1903.

2. "From an Adobe Hut."

3. "From an Adobe Hut."

4. "From an Adobe Hut."

5. "From an Adobe Hut." The better-known account of this experience comes from Susa Young Gates, *Memorial to Elizabeth Claridge McCune: Missionary, Philanthropist, Architect* (Salt Lake City, UT: n.p., 1924), but the account in *the Deseret Evening News* is much earlier and less heavily edited, thus preserving Elizabeth's voice more accurately.

6. "From an Adobe Hut."

7. "From an Adobe Hut."

8. Gates, *Memorial*, 17.

9. Gates, *Memorial*, 84.

Chapter 8 · Sarah Louisa Yates Robison

1. Louise Yates Robison, Address, March 1944, Relief Society Birthday Party, Sunset Ward, San Francisco Stake, Typescript, p. 3, Gladys R. Winter Scrapbooks, Church History Library, The Church of Jesus Christ of Latter-day Saints, Salt Lake City, Utah.

2. Robison, Address, March 1944, 5.

3. Janet Peterson and LaRene Gaunt, *Faith, Hope, and Charity* (American Fork, UT: Covenant Communications, 2008), 124.

4. Gladys R. Winter, "Mother in Her Home," p. 7, Gladys R. Winter Scrapbooks, Church History Library.

5. Winter, "Mother in Her Home," 7.

6. Gladys R. Winter, "Mother in the General Presidency of the Relief Society," Gladys R. Winter Scrapbooks, p. [1], Church History Library.

7. Winter, "Mother in the General Presidency," [1].

8. Winter, "Mother in the General Presidency," [1].

9. "The Fundamental Purpose of Our Work Days," *Relief Society Magazine* 23 (January 1936): 51.

10. "Sister Louise Y. Robison," Conference Report, October 1929, 84.

11. Peterson and Gaunt, *Faith, Hope and Charity*, 132–33.

12. Belle S. Spafford Oral History, Interviews by Jill Mulvay Derr, 1975–76, Typescript, p. 40, James Moyle Oral History Program, Church History Library.

Chapter 9 · Amanda Barnes Smith

1. Hulda Cordelia Thurston Smith, "O My Children and Grandchildren," in *Nauvoo Journal* 4, no. 2 (Fall 1992): 5. Cordelia (the name she went by) married Willard G. Smith, the eldest child of Warren and Amanda. In her narrative, Cordelia stated that years later Amanda acted as proxy in the baptism of the woman and had her sealed to Warren.

2. Amanda Barnes Smith, quoted in Emmeline B. Wells, "Amanda Smith," *Woman's Exponent* 9, no. 21 (April 1, 1881): 165.

3. Amanda Barnes Smith, History, Photocopy of holograph, p. 3, L. Tom Perry Special Collections, Harold B. Lee Library, Brigham Young University, Provo, Utah.

4. Smith, quoted in Wells, "Amanda Smith,"165; Amanda Barnes Smith, quoted in Emmeline B. Wells, "Amanda Smith," *Woman's Exponent* 9, no. 22 (April 15, 1881): 173.

5. Smith, quoted in Wells, "Amanda Smith," 173.

6. Smith, quoted in Wells, "Amanda Smith," 173.

7. Amanda Barnes Smith, quoted in Edward W. Tullidge, *The Women of Mormondom* (New York: Tullidge & Crandall, 1877), 123–24, 128.

8. See Mosiah 24:10–11.

9. Smith, quoted in Tullidge, *Women of Mormondom*, 129.

10. Smith, quoted in Tullidge, *Women of Mormondom*, 129–30. The lines come from the seventh stanza of the hymn "How Firm a Foundation," included in the 1835 Latter-day Saint hymnal *A Collection of Sacred Hymns for the Church of the Latter Day Saints* (Kirtland, Ohio: F. G. Williams & Co., 1835), 112–13; see also *Hymns of The Church of Jesus Christ of Latter-day Saints* (Salt Lake City: The Church of Jesus Christ of Latter-day Saints, 1985), no. 85.

11. Amanda Barnes Smith, quoted in Emmeline B. Wells, "Amanda Smith," *Woman's Exponent* 10, no. 2 (June 15, 1881): 13; spelling modernized.

CHAPTER 10 · LUCY HANNAH WHITE FLAKE

1. Lucy H. Flake, Journals, 1894–1899, 3 vols., Holograph, 1:8–9, L. Tom Perry Special Collections, Harold B. Lee Library, Brigham Young University, Provo, Utah; spelling, punctuation, and capitalization modernized in quotations from this document.

2. Flake, Journals, 1:3.

3. Flake, Journals, 2:71, May 16, 1896.

4. Flake, Journals, 1:9.

5. Flake, Journals, 1:9.

6. Flake, Journals, 1:9–10.

7. Flake, Journals, 1:9–10.

8. Osmer D. Flake, *William J. Flake: Pioneer-Colonizer* (Phoenix, AZ: n.p., 1948), 56.

9. Flake, Journals, 1:19.

10. Flake, Journals, 1:22.

11. Roberta Flake Clayton, *To the Last Frontier: Autobiography of Lucy Hanna White Flake* (Mesa, AZ: n.p., 1923), 68–69.

12. Flake, Journals, 2:28, June 16, 1895.

CHAPTER 11 · SARAH ANN NELSON PETERSON

1. Canute Peterson, "The Story of Canute Peterson As Told to His Daughter Carrie," *Instructor* 81, no. 4 (April 1946): 174.

2. Anthon H. Lund, "A Noble Life," *Latter-day Saints' Millennial Star* 58, no. 27 (July 2, 1896): 428.

3. Hamilton Gardner, *History of Lehi* (Salt Lake City, UT: Deseret News, 1913), 88–89.

4. Canute Peterson to Sarah A. Peterson, August 13, 1856, quoted in Carrie Peterson Tanner, "Story of the Life of Canute Peterson As Given by Himself and by Some Members of His Family," Appendix: Letter 9, Typescript, private possession.
5. Lund, "Noble Life," 429.
6. "Minutes of Quarterly Conference of the Y.L.M.I.A.," *Young Woman's Journal* 1, no. 2 (November 1889): 51.

CHAPTER 12 · ANNA KARINE GAARDEN WIDTSOE

1. John A. Widtsoe, *In the Gospel Net: The Story of Anna Karine Gaarden Widtsoe* (Salt Lake City, Utah: Improvement Era, 1942), 60–61.
2. Widtsoe, *In the Gospel Net*, 65.
3. Widtsoe, *In the Gospel Net*, 67.
4. Widtsoe, *In the Gospel Net*, 67–68.
5. Andrew Jenson, Remarks, "Funeral Services of Mrs. Anna K. Widtsoe," July 13, 1919, Typescript, p. 13, Widtsoe Family Papers, 1824–1953, Church History Library, The Church of Jesus Christ of Latter-day Saints, Salt Lake City, Utah.
6. Widtsoe, *Gospel Net*, 105–6.
7. Widtsoe, *Gospel Net*, 116.
8. Albert E. Bowen, Remarks, "Funeral Services for Sister Petroline Gaarden," April 14, 1929, Widtsoe Family Papers, Church History Library.
9. Widtsoe, *Gospel Net*, 116.

CHAPTER 13 · MAUD MAY BABCOCK

1. "Babcock Resigns as 'U' Speech Head," *Utah Daily Chronicle*, April 21, 1938.
2. Herbert B. Maw, Remarks at Maud May Babcock Celebration, October 8, 1981, Babcock Reading Arts Society, Maud May Babcock Papers, Special Collections, J. Willard Marriott Library, University of Utah, Salt Lake City, Utah.
3. Maw, Remarks.
4. Maw, Remarks.
5. Maw, Remarks.
6. "Officers' Notes: Hints on Presenting a Lesson to Juniors," *Young Woman's Journal* 20, no. 7 (July 1909): 341–42.
7. Maw, Remarks.

CHAPTER 14 · LOUISA GRANT ALSTON

1. Lorenzo Snow to William Pierson, May 25, 1899, quoted in Melvin S. Tagg, *A History of the Mormon Church in Canada* (Lethbridge, Alberta: Lethbridge Herald, 1968), 66.
2. "Pioneer History of Magrath: Joseph Alston and Family," Typescript, p. 1, Mormon Pioneers Genealogical Project, Glenbow Museum Archives, Calgary, Alberta; spelling modernized in quotations from this document.
3. Jane Alston, "The History of Joseph William Alston," student paper, Lethbridge Community College, Lethbridge, Alberta, 1971, 2.
4. "Pioneer History," 1–2.
5. Louisa Grant Alston, "Louisa Grant Alston," Typescript, p. 1, Mormon Pioneers Genealogical Project, Glenbow Museum Archives.
6. "Magrath Boy Scouts Sponsor Successful Banquet for Fathers," *Lethbridge Herald*, April 2, 1930.
7. "Service Recognized," *Lethbridge Herald*, February 26, 1940.

8. Alston, "Louisa Grant Alston," 2.

9. Edward W. Beatty to Louisa Alston, March 14, 1939, Canadian General Council, Boy Scouts Association of Canada, private possession.

CHAPTER 15 • BELINDA MARDEN PRATT

1. Belinda Marden Pratt, Autobiography, 1884, Holograph, Church History Library, The Church of Jesus Christ of Latter-day Saints, Salt Lake City, Utah.

2. Pratt, Autobiography, 1884; syntax modernized.

3. Pratt, Autobiography, 1884.

4. Pratt, Autobiography, 1884.

5. Pratt, Autobiography, 1884; spelling and grammar modernized.

6. Pratt, Autobiography, 1884.

7. Pratt, Autobiography, 1884.

8. Pratt, Autobiography, 1884.

9. Ann Agatha Walker Pratt, Journal, quoted in "Parley P. Pratt: His Twelve Wives," in *Our Pioneer Heritage*, ed. Kate B. Carter, vol. 17 (Salt Lake City, Utah: Daughters of Utah Pioneers, 1974), 231.

10. Belinda Marden Pratt to Lydia Kimball, January 12, 1854. Transcription available at http://jared.pratt-family.org/parley_family_histories/belinda_marden_defense.html.

11. "Belinda Marden Pratt Biography," in *History and Genealogy of the Franklin Alonzo Robison Family,* comp. Carrie Robison Despain and Melba Despain Garner, 1960, Jared Pratt Family Association website, accessed September 18, 2015, http://jared .pratt-family.org/parley_family_histories/belinda_marden_biography_2.html.

CHAPTER 16 • ELIZABETH HARRISON GODDARD

1. Elizabeth Harrison Goddard, Autobiography, Holograph, p. 58, Church History Library; spelling and punctuation modernized in quotations from this document.

2. E. H. Goddard, Autobiography, 59.

3. George Goddard, "Autobiography," in *Our Pioneer Heritage*, ed. Kate B. Carter, vol. 13 (Salt Lake City, Utah: Daughters of Utah Pioneers, 1970), 458.

4. E. H. Goddard, Autobiography, 61.

5. E. H. Goddard, Autobiography, 61.

6. E. H. Goddard, Autobiography, 62.

7. E. H. Goddard, Autobiography, 62.

8. E. H. Goddard, Autobiography, 63.

9. G. Goddard, "Autobiography," 460.

10. G. Goddard, "Review of an Active Life," *Juvenile Instructor* 17 (March 1, 1882): 76.

11. E. H. Goddard, Autobiography, 64.

12. E. H. Goddard, Autobiography, 64.

13. G. Goddard, "Autobiography," 461; "Notice," *Deseret News Weekly*, October 29, 1853.

14. E. H. Goddard, Autobiography, 65.

15. Emmeline B. Wells, "In Memoriam: Elizabeth H. Goddard," *Woman's Exponent* 31 (May 1903): 92.

CHAPTER 17 • RACHEL EMMA WOOLLEY SIMMONS

1. Rachel Emma Woolley Simmons, Journal, vol. 1, Holograph, p. 2, Rachel W. Simmons Collection, Church History Library, The Church of Jesus Christ of

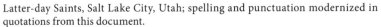

Latter-day Saints, Salt Lake City, Utah; spelling and punctuation modernized in quotations from this document.

2. Simmons, Journal, 1:30.

3. Rachel Emma Simmons Willes, "Biography of My Mother, Rachel Emma Woolley Simmons," 1925, Typescript, p. 1, private possession.

4. Simmons, Journal, 1:49.

5. Simmons, Journal, 1:57–58.

6. Simmons, Journal, 1:87, 89.

7. Simmons, Journal, 1:97.

8. Rachel Emma Woolley Simmons, Journal, vol. 2, June 30, 1883, Holograph, pp. 94–95, Rachel W. Simmons Collection, Church History Library; spelling and punctuation modernized in quotations from this document.

9. Joseph Willes, "Brief Biography of Rachel Emma Woolley Simmons," ca. 1947, Typescript, p. 34, Church History Library.

10. Simmons, Journal, February 1, 1883, 2:69.

11. Willes, "Brief Biography," 1, 83.

Chapter 18 · Janetta Ann McBride Ferrin

1. Janetta Ann McBride Ferrin quoted in Ethel Ferrin Davis [granddaughter], "Story of Janetta Ann McBride Ferrin," ca. 1924, Typescript, p. 8, private possession.

2. Janetta Ann McBride Ferrin, "Personal History," 1924, Typescript, p. 3, private possession; spelling, capitalization, and punctuation modernized in quotations from this document.

3. Davis, "Story of Janetta," 8, 10.

4. Janetta A. McBride Ferrin, "Personal History," 1924, Typescript, p. 4, private possession.

5. Heber Robert McBride, "Autobiography," ca. 1868, Typescript, pp. 10–11, Church History Library, The Church of Jesus Christ of Latter-day Saints, Salt Lake City, Utah; spelling, grammar, and punctuation modernized.

6. Janetta Ann McBride Ferrin, "Autobiographical Sketch," 1924, Typescript, p. 2, private possession; spelling and punctuation modernized.

7. Laura McBride Smith [Peter's daughter], "The Story of My Grandfather: Peter Howard McBride," Typescript, p. 5, International Society Daughters of Utah Pioneers (DUP), Salt Lake City, Utah; punctuation modernized in quotations from this document.

8. Gladys McBride Stewart, "Peter Howard McBride," Typescript, p. 2, DUP; spelling modernized.

9. Heber McBride to Zelma McBride Ririe West, May 13, 1923, in "Heber McBride: From the Personal History of Zelma McBride Ririe West," Typescript, p. 1, DUP.

10. Ferrin, "Personal History," 3.

11. Smith, "Story of My Grandfather," 5.

12. Davis, "Story of Janetta," 11.

13. Ether Enos McBride, "Autobiographical Sketch," Typescript, p. 4, DUP.

14. Janetta Ann McBride Ferrin, "My Life with My Husband," dictated to daughter Sarah Elizabeth Ferrin Lines, pp. 1–2, available at DUP, Pioneer Memorial Museum, Salt Lake City, Utah.

Contributors

WILLIAM RAY ALSTON has two degrees from the University of Lethbridge and has taught school in southern Alberta, Canada, for over thirty years. William and his wife, Susan, live in Magrath, Alberta, Canada, and have four children and thirteen grandchildren. Louisa Grant Alston is William's great-grandmother.

ALEXANDER L. BAUGH is a professor of Church history and doctrine at Brigham Young University. He received his BS from Utah State University and his MA and PhD in history from BYU. He serves as co-director of research for the Religious Studies Center at BYU and is a volume editor for the Joseph Smith Papers. He and his wife, Susan, are the parents of five children and reside in Highland, Utah.

DAVID F. BOONE received an MA in frontier-American western history and a PhD in educational leadership, both from Brigham Young University, where he teaches religion. David and his wife, Mary, are the parents of eight children and grandparents to twenty-three. A great-grandson of Lucy Hannah White Flake, he is transcribing and annotating her journals for publication.

CHRISTINE BANKS BOWERS received a BS in sociology from the University of Utah and an MA in marriage, family, and child counseling from the University of Nevada–Reno. She has worked as a therapist and educator and lives in Maui, Hawaii, with her husband, Daniel, a great-grandson of Mary Goble Pay. They are the parents of two children and grandparents of five.

CLINTON D. CHRISTENSEN received a BA and MA in English from Brigham Young University. He also earned a master's degree in library and information science from Wayne State University. He works in the LDS Church History Department and specializes in international Church history. He and his wife and two sons live in Willard, Utah.

CAROL L. CLARK holds a PhD from the University of Utah and is retired from the LDS Family History Department. She has won national awards for her writing and served on the Relief Society general board under three presidents. Laura Clark Phelps is Carol's great-great-great aunt.

REBEKAH RYAN CLARK graduated from Harvard University with a BA in American history and literature and received a JD from the J. Reuben Clark School of Law at Brigham Young University. Rebekah and her husband, Andrew, live in Highland, Utah, with their four children. She and her brother, coauthor Marcus Patrick Ryan, are great-great-great-grandchildren of Janetta Ann McBride Ferrin.

DAVID R. COOK earned a BS in chemistry from the University of Utah and an MBA from Westminster College (Salt Lake City). His career has taken him from laboratory science to public health. He and his wife, Kristin, have four daughters. He is a descendant of Susanah Stone Lloyd.

JEFF HILLAM received a BA in Jewish studies at Purdue University and an MBA from the Thunderbird School of Global Management. He owns and operates a management consulting company. He and his wife, Alisha, and their three children live in the greater Boston area. He is the great-great-great-grandson of Mary Roselia Cook McCann.

JENNIFER L. LUND is the director of the Historic Sites Division of the LDS Church History Department. She received a BA in English from the University of Utah and an MA in American history from Brigham Young University. Her husband, Anthony, is a great-great-grandson of Sarah Ann Nelson Peterson.

MATTHEW S. McBRIDE earned a BS in business management from the University of Utah and is pursuing an MA in history at the same institution. A web strategist for the LDS Church History Department, he wrote *A House for the Most High: The Story of the Original Nauvoo Temple* (2007). He lives in American Fork, Utah, with his wife, Mary, and their four children.

MARJORIE NEWTON earned her BA, MA (Hons.), and PhD from the University of Sydney. She is the author of *Southern Cross Saints: The Mormons in Australia* (1991), *Hero or Traitor? A Biographical Study of Charles Wesley Wandell* (1992), *Tiki and Temple: The Mormon Mission in New Zealand, 1854–1958* (2012), and *Mormon and Maori* (2014), as well as numerous articles. Marjorie is an Australian who was born in Sydney and lives in Hobart, Tasmania.

Catherine Wheelwright Ockey received a BA in English and history from Brigham Young University. She and her husband raised their children on an island off the coast of Washington, where she also worked as a freelance writer and newspaper reporter. Now she writes from her home in Helena, Montana. She is a great-great-great-granddaughter of Diantha Morley Billings.

Kiersten Olson earned a BA in music from Brigham Young University. She served a mission in Norway, where she developed a deep respect for the Widtsoe family. Kiersten is pursuing an MA in history at the University of Utah and works as an administrative assistant at the LDS Church History Library. She lives in Cottonwood Heights, Utah.

Madelyn Stewart Silver Palmer graduated from Wellesley College with a degree in psychobiology and studied medicine at the University of Utah Medical School. She practices medicine in Littleton, Colorado, and is the author of *Elinore's Choice* (2013). She and her husband, James, are the parents of four sons.

Virginia H. Pearce received a BA in history and a master's degree in social work, both from the University of Utah. She has worked as a therapist and written several books. Virginia served on the Primary general board and as a counselor in the Young Women general presidency. She and her late husband, James, are the parents of six children and grandparents of twenty-seven. She is the great-granddaughter of Mary Goble Pay.

Taunalyn Ford Rutherford received a BA in history and an MA in humanities from Brigham Young University. She is a doctoral candidate in religious studies at Claremont Graduate University and is an adjunct instructor of religion at Brigham Young University. Taunalyn and her husband, James, are the parents of five children and reside in Draper, Utah.

Marcus Patrick Ryan earned a BA in political science from Brigham Young University and a JD from the University of Texas School of Law. He and his wife, Stephanie, live in Austin, Texas, and have three children. Marcus and his sister, coauthor Rebekah Ryan Clark, are great-great-great-grandchildren of Janetta Ann McBride Ferrin.

Patricia Lemmon Spilsbury received a BA in English and journalism from the University of Arizona and an MA in curriculum and instruction from the University of Nevada–Las Vegas. She taught school in Las Vegas, where she raised seven children. She is the grandmother of thirteen and serves as a Church service missionary in the LDS Church History Library.

Patricia H. Stoker received a BA from the University of Utah. She has served as a member of Church curriculum writing committees and provided research for *To the Rescue: The Biography of Thomas S. Monson*. Patricia and her husband, Stephen, live in Salt Lake City. They are the parents of seven children and grandparents of twenty-seven. Patricia is the great-granddaughter of Mary Goble Pay.

Laurel Thatcher Ulrich received a BA in English from the University of Utah, an MA in English from Simmons College (Boston), and a PhD in history from the University of New Hampshire. She and her husband, Gael, live in Cambridge, Massachusetts, where she is a member of the faculty at Harvard University. She grew up hearing stories about Maud May Babcock because her father, John Kenneth Thatcher, was a member of the Babcock Varsity Players in the 1920s.

Laura F. Willes holds a BA in American studies from the University of Minnesota. She is the author of four books: *Minnesota Mormons* (1990), *Community of Faith* (2000), *Christmas with the Prophets* (2010), and *Miracle in the Pacific* (2012). She and her husband, Mark, are the parents of five children and grandparents of twenty.

Image Credits

Except as noted, images are courtesy Church History Library, The Church of Jesus Christ of Latter-day Saints, Salt Lake City, Utah. All images are used by permission.

Page

xvi. Johnny Adolphson/Shutterstock

1. *Susanah Stone Lloyd*. Courtesy International Society Daughters of Utah Pioneers.

3. smcfeeters/Shutterstock.

4. Robyn Mackenzie/Shutterstock.

6. ImagesbyInfinity/Shutterstock.

7. *Laura Clark Phelps*. Sketch by Stephanie Weber. Courtesy Mabel R. Whitmore.

9. *Courthouse in Richmond, Missouri, ca. 1870*. Courtesy Church History Library.

14. dancha/iStock.

15. *Rosa Clara Friedlander Logie*. Marjorie B. Newton, "Australia's Pioneer Saints," *Ensign*, February 1997, 47, public domain.

17. Abeleao/iStock.

20. *San Francisco Harbor, ca. 1850*. Courtesy Library of Congress.

24. Laurie Partridge/Shutterstock.

25. *Mary Roselia Cook McCann*. Courtesy International Society Daughters of Utah Pioneers.

26. *Two young women on the shores of Bear Lake, 1911*. Courtesy Idaho State Historical Society, Browsing Collection 72-189-134.

30. hilaryfox/iStock.

31. *Mary Goble Pay*. Courtesy Patricia H. Stoker.

33. *Wagon train in Echo Canyon, 1867*. Courtesy Church History Library.

34. *Mary Goble Pay and her husband, Richard Pay*. Courtesy Church History Library.

36. madsci/iStock.

38. base1101658/Shutterstock.

39. *Diantha Morley Billings*. Courtesy International Society Daughters of Utah Pioneers.

44. *McCune Mansion, 1917*. Courtesy Church History Library.

45. *Elizabeth Ann Claridge McCune*. Special Collections & Archives, Merrill-Cazier Library, Utah State University, Logan, Utah.
47. microstocker/iStock.
48. *Alfred and Elizabeth McCune*. Special Collections & Archives, Merrill-Cazier Library, Utah State University, Logan, Utah.
52. Bejim/Shutterstock.
53. *Sarah Louisa Yates Robison*. Courtesy Church History Library.
56. Julie Ardaran/Shutterstock.
58. *Stone from Haun's Mill, Missouri*. Courtesy Americasroof/Wikimedia
59. *Amanda Barnes Smith*. Courtesy Church History Library.
64. *Snowflake Arizona Temple*. Courtesy sgilsdorf/Wikimedia
65. *Lucy Hannah White Flake*. Courtesy David F. Boone.
67. Andyworks/iStock.
69. *William Flake*. Courtesy Church History Library.
70. Maxim Gostev/iStock.
71. *Sarah Ann Nelson Peterson*. Courtesy Church History Library.
74. ZargoDesign/iStock.
78. *Frøya, Norway*. Courtesy Alask Raanes/Wikimedia
79. *Anna Karine Gaarden Widtsoe*. Courtesy Church History Library.
81. diphot06/iStock.
85. *Anna Widtsoe and sons, ca. 1883*. Courtesy Church History Library.
86. shemara/iStock.
87. *Maud May Babcock*. Courtesy Special Collections Department, J. Willard Marriott Library, University of Utah.
90. *Alston Scout Park*. Courtesy William Ray Alston.
91. *Louisa Grant Alston*. Courtesy William Ray Alston.
93. Grash Alex/Shutterstock.
98. Wessel du Plooy/Shutterstock.
99. *Belinda Marden Pratt*. Courtesy Church History Library.
100. Greg Kushmerek/Shutterstock.
103. *Parley P. Pratt and Belinda Marden Pratt*. Courtesy Church History Library.
104. Shauna Gibby/Deseret Book
105. *Elizabeth Harrison Goddard*. Courtesy Church History Library.
107. Alphotographic/iStock.
109. Denice Breaux/iStock.
110. *George Godddard*. Courtesy Church History Library.
112. BanksPhotos/iStock.
113. *Rachel Emma Woolley Simmons*. Courtesy Laura F. Willes.
116. *Rachel Emma Woolley Simmons with grandchildren, ca. 1880*. Courtesy Church History Library.
118. Vladimir Salman/Shutterstock.
119. *Janetta Ann McBride Ferrin*. Courtesy International Society Daughters of Utah Pioneers.
Part pages: Rodin Olena/Shutterstock

Index